— DEMOCRACY MUST WORK —

A TRILATERAL AGENDA FOR THE DECADE

A Task Force Report
to the Trilateral Commission

Authors:

DAVID OWEN
Member of British Parliament;
Leader of the Social Democratic Party;
Former Foreign Secretary

ZBIGNIEW BRZEZINSKI
Herbert Lehman Professor of Government,
Columbia University;
Senior Advisor, Georgetown University Center
for Strategic & International Studies;
Former Assistant to the President
for National Security Affairs

SABURO OKITA
Chairman,
Institute for Domestic & International Policy Studies;
Former Japanese Foreign Minister

Associate Authors:

MICHAEL STEWART
Reader in Political Economy,
University College, London

CAROL RAE HANSEN
Department of Government,
Harvard University

Published by
NEW YORK UNIVERSITY PRESS
New York and London
1984

This report was prepared for the Trilateral Commission and is released
under its auspices. It was discussed at the Trilateral Commission meeting
in Washington on April 1-3, 1984. The authors, who are experts from
Western Europe, North America and Japan, have been free to present
their own views; and the opinions expressed are put forth in a personal
capacity and do not purport to represent those of the Commission or of
any organization with which the authors are associated. The Commission
is making this report available for wider distribution as a contribution to
informed discussion and handling of the issues treated.

Library of Congress Cataloging in Publication Data
Owen, David, 1938–
  Democracy must work

    (The Triangle papers; 28)
    1. International economic relations. 2. International relations. 3. Manpower policy.
    I. Okita, Saburo, 1914–   II. Brzezinski, Zbigniew K., 1928–   III. Trilateral Commis-
    sion. IV. Title. V. Series.
HF1411.094 1984   337   84-2499
ISBN 0-8147-6160-7
ISBN 0-8147-6161-5 (pbk.)
  Manufactured in the United States of America

Table of Contents

I. Dilemmas of the Decade

For the first time in history, a truly global world system is emerging. Jet travel, communications satellites and computers have shrunk the planet to an extent scarcely imaginable only a few decades ago. The opportunity for an entirely new system of global cooperation is there to be seized.

Yet, also for the first time, dangers of a truly global dimension now confront mankind. Broadly speaking, these dangers are derived from the unprecedented scientific-technological capacity now available for inflicting worldwide devastation and death; and from the risk that regional social and economic breakdowns will overload a still rudimentary structure of international cooperation, prompting massive suffering, political conflicts, and eventually global chaos.

Specifically, the principal threats confronting the global community can be considered in the following descending order of physical destructiveness, but in ascending order of probability of actual occurrence during the next decade:

1. Nuclear war, with its unprecedented capacity for limitless death and destruction, a catastrophe from which our globe might not recover.

2. Major social breakdowns in large portions of Africa, Asia and perhaps Latin America. Large-scale famines, massive population migrations, and chaotic violence could be involved, reducing prospects for democracy and enhancing the opportunities for extremists of the left and right to seize power.

3. Increasingly destructive regional conflicts, less and less susceptible to international containment, carrying with them the growing risk of East-West confrontations.

4. Significant deterioration in multilateral economic and political cooperation, rising unemployment, lower living standards and less democracy.

However, it would be wrong to draw only an apocalyptic scenario. Our era's future is ambivalent because the negative trends identified above conflict with significant opportunities. The more hopeful global trends include:

1. The beginnings of global strategies for international cooperation, including some cases of effective performance on the part of functional global institutions in economic development and peacekeeping.

2. The potential for a more intelligent management of global affairs through scientific and technical breakthroughs in medicine, communications, and nutrition, among others.

3. The decline in the appeal of the Soviet model of development, particularly in the Third World.

4. The compelling nature of freedom and of human rights.

In effect, the gradual degradation of international order, though possible, is not historically inevitable. If the 1980s prove to be a decade out of control, it will be because the trilateral countries will have failed fully to exploit the potential for progress that does in fact exist. Global anarchy and international violence will then be the inexcusable legacies of a failure of will on the part of the richest, the most productive, and the most democratic sectors of the globe.

When the Trilateral Commission was founded in 1973 with representatives from Western Europe, Japan and North America, the key issue was how to shape trilateral relations so that Japan could be integrated as a coequal partner with what until then had been largely a bilateral Atlantic relationship. This aim did not prove easy to accomplish. In Europe the objectives of the Commission were often misunderstood, particularly by the political left. In the United States, by contrast, the main critics were on the right. The European left saw it as aimed at protecting the capitalist military status quo, insensitive to North-South concerns, and resistant to easing East-West tensions. The American right saw the Commission's internationalist outlook as a threat to the assertion of America's nationhood. Above all there was in Europe at that time too little understanding of the potential and extent of the scientific and technological revolution that Japan was spearheading, which has now made her the world leader in many of the technologies of the future. The growing importance and influence in the United States of its southern and western states was also not forseen early enough in Europe. These states, not as Euro-centered as the Eastern Seaboard states and historically more orientated towards Latin America and across the Pacific for their overseas trade, have become more significant politically and economically.

In the next decade, with the growing importance for the United States of the Pacific connection, and with Europe in grave danger of failing to develop its economic potential and political unity, the difficulty will be how to keep the Atlantic and Pacific connections in balance.

The problem is an acute one. Up to 1973 the European economy grew at a significantly faster rate than the American economy. But it has slowed down drastically in the last few years and failed to create new jobs. Between 1973 and 1983 employment in the European Community countries actually fell by 3 million whereas in the United States it increased by 13 million. Nineteen eighty-four looks like being the 12th consecutive year in which unemployment in Europe rose.

Wage-earners in Europe, despite the two oil shocks of 1973 and 1979, have managed to maintain the increase in their purchasing power, in spite of the slow-down in growth, far more than in the United States or Japan. But this European preference for consumption has led to low profitability, low investment and to the inhibition of economic growth. There is also a growing technological gap between Europe on the one hand and the United States and Japan on the other. Meanwhile, the cost of social services in Europe has been rising considerably faster than national income.

The European Community needs to find a way out of this vicious circle without delay. Many of those to whom we have talked in the course of preparing this report take a gloomy view of Europe's future, arguing that apathy and fatalism are gaining ground and that there is too little willingness to make the effort to put things right. We think that this view is too pessimistic, and that—given the will—Europe has the capacity to play a full role in the new technological age. But a fundamental part of our analysis is that Europe cannot recover by itself. It needs the stimulation of a coordinated international recovery as part of a comprehensive global economic, political and strategic reassessment.

We cannot chart a coherent constructive path for the trilateral countries for the next decade without examining carefully the crucial trends which are at work. Just examining trends within the trilateral countries would be insufficient; we need to understand the trends which challenge all countries, not just our own. Some of these trends are economic, some social, and some political. Some are beneficial. Others are ominous. Some can be readily documented with statistics. Others are more elusive. But they are all of great importance. A few are to be welcomed and encouraged. Others threaten a slide into increasing misery and chaos—unless appropriate action is taken in time.

Numerous reports and books have been written, and seminars held, foretelling the future in many of our countries, yet they have had little impact. There has been an initial flurry of publicity and apparent interest, perhaps, but little follow through or lasting effect. Doom-laden forecasts, exaggerated language and an obsession with proposing new structures and institutions have meant that much wisdom and careful analysis have been lost sight of by key decision makers because of the atmosphere of unreality initially created which has allowed much good sense to be disparaged and defeated.

The task we have set ourselves is to analyze carefully the trends which can give a reasonable basis for projection over the next decade and to try to propose achievable objectives and realistic methods of modifying and building on those trends for the future. We propose global solutions but concentrate our attention on trilateral action, not because we believe that global action is not needed but because it is a formidable enough task to achieve a consensus on what the trilateral countries should do. It is also within these countries that this report has the greatest chance of achieving results. We have deliberately adopted an incremental approach, eschewing grandiose strategies, in the belief that a series of coordinated actions taken in good time can in combination provide a powerful agenda for the trilateral countries to contribute to the global good.

We focus our recommendations on the summits of seven trilateral countries. We think it best to consider a program covering the next several summits, with the hope of achieving a global recovery sustainable through the 1990s.

It is obvious that there will be differences of view even within the trilateral countries on what constitutes the global good. In our recommendations, we give the highest priority to the maintenance and the extension of democracy. In this report, we are concerned with the trilateral industrial democracies. We recognize that there are democracies in the developing world, but their capabilities and needs are quite different from those of the industrialized West, and thus are not specifically discussed in this report. We see the essential freedom of democracy to be broadly incompatible with a state controlled economy and we are not afraid to openly reject communism and to attempt to devise a global system where the communist philosophy withers and has no new converts.

For this to happen those who extol the merits of democracy have a special responsibility to ensure that democracy works: "works" in the sense that democratic government can be efficient in its use of resources, yet fair and just in the distribution of rewards; "works" in the sense that all the citizens who want to contribute to society by working, can work. That is not an easy combination to achieve. The market economy, though far preferable to the state-run economy, does need some degree of modification if it is to be successful in providing all its citizens with a reasonable standard of living and the opportunity to work. It must also display a greater degree of awareness of the economic and political needs of citizens in other countries.

In 1975 a report on the governability of democracies, *The Crisis of Democracy*, was presented to the Trilateral Commission. It talked of a "consensus without purpose" and said that without a common purpose there is no basis for common priorities. Nine years later, having survived many crises, we believe that the democracies have shown a remarkable resilience. We are not depressed about the governability of democracy. Our greatest concern lies in the inability of the democracies to share a common purpose in combining, coordinating and developing internationally.

Democracy does not work of itself but it provides the framework for society, the basic organization and structure within which individuals can live freely with the minimum of constraints necessary to protect the public good. At the same time, a democratic government must respond to the pressures which arise from the needs and wishes of its people.

One such pressure on democratic government is the old age dependency ratio which, while showing little change in developing countries, in developed countries is expected to rise by a third between 1970 and 2000; in Japan it is expected to double. The proportion of the population in developed countries aged 80 and over will also continue to rise sharply; in the twenty-four OECD countries there were 12 million people in this category in 1970, nearly 16 million in 1980, and will be nearly 21 million by 1990. This rising proportion of old people in the population will tend to raise transfer payments, such as old age pensions, and social service expenditures as a proportion of GDP in developed countries. Over the next decade or two the financing of these expenditures will become an increasingly critical issue.

Another serious problem is the present level of unemployment, particularly in Europe. Not only is this economically wasteful and socially disruptive; it also constitutes a political danger, a threat to the viability of democracy. It is necessary for those of us committed to democratic government to remember that communist countries, for all the inefficiencies of their economies, do provide more jobs for their citizens. These factors are dealt with in Chapter II, *Employment and Equity*.

In Western democracies, where governments are bound by the rule of law, and required to seek re-election at fairly frequent intervals, an important aspect of the working of democracy is the relationship between the powers of the central government on the one hand, and the powers of regional or local government on the other. Among the trilateral countries there are those—such as the United States and Germany—which have federal governments and those—such as Britain and Japan—which have unitary governments. But the essential tensions between central and local government—between centralization and decentralization—exist regardless of constitutional structure.

Over the past few decades pressures have developed in many democratic countries for a greater degree of decentralization. This was partly a reaction to the growth of the cost of, and interference by, central bureaucracies during the war—and in some cases post-war—years; and partly a reflection of rising levels of income, education and leisure and the impetus this gave towards a greater degree of autonomy on the part of individual regions and localities as well as to greater control by individuals over their working lives and environments, leading to pressure for more industrial democracy and more say by local residents' associations in decisions which affected their locality. Although basically a thoroughly desirable trend, it must not be lost sight of that in some cases this decentralization of power has made it easier for particular interest groups to block progress.

Over the next decade the devolution of power from the center will need to be consistent with another likely and desirable trend: a greater degree of policy coordination on economic matters. Governments that see the need to devolve more decisions to regional and local levels will need to ensure that this does not conflict with macroeconomic commitments to a better international economic order.

The last twenty years have witnessed a substantial increase in the interdependence of the world economy, with world trade rising considerably faster than world output, the external public and private debt of developing countries rising at a rapid rate, particularly since 1973, and the virtual absence of exchange controls in the main trilateral countries permitting short-term capital flows from one country to another which can overwhelm official attempts to maintain an orderly exchange rate regime. These issues are covered in Chapter III, *Interdependence and Growth*, where it is argued that if the trilateral countries can achieve a sustained growth rate this will make manageable the problem of indebtedness, and that in order to achieve this growth a greater measure of exchange rate stability would be helpful.

Yet despite increased interdependence, nationalism remains a potent force within many countries—including some trilateral countries—as minorities with a strong sense of religious or cultural identity have attempted to push the desire for devolution to the point of secession. Nationalism has also been fuelled, as in the past, by economic depression, which provides an emotional cover for "beggar-thy-neighbor" policies, and often feeds on an incipient militarism. Attempts to dilute the force of nationalism by establishing regional groupings dealing with economic, political or security cooperation have met with mixed success. Much the most ambitious attempt was the creation in 1957 of the European Economic Community. It still has not fulfilled the aspirations of its founders. Although the elimination of tariff barriers within Western Europe led to a rapid growth in trade and stimulated faster growth during the 1960s and early 1970s, divergence of national interests within the Community has resulted in it being much less effective in tackling the problems of the 1980s. Industries with large amounts of excess capacity, such as steel and shipbuilding, have been contracted only slowly and after much argument; the Common Agricultural Policy seems as far from radical reform as ever; and rivalry between the governments and big firms of the individual countries means that Europe is falling dangerously behind the United States and Japan in the development and application of the technologies of the future.

On the security front, the trilateral democracies have remained solid, despite the withdrawal from the NATO military organization of France—a step perhaps more symbolic than real. But the cohesiveness of the West as a whole worldwide has been reduced, compared with twenty years ago, by the fading of the post-war American hegemony, the increasing economic frictions between the three trilateral partners, and growing doubts in Western Europe about American nuclear defense policies. These issues are covered in more detail in Chapter IV, *Cooperation or Fragmentation*, where the degree of security interdependence is charted both in terms of the trilateral countries and globally.

But if the world is to prosper, if the democracies are to flourish, and if more countries are to achieve democratic government over the next decade, then national governments, particularly those of the main trilateral countries, will have to take more account of the interdependence of their decision making. Closer coordination of macroeconomic policies is called for, along the lines attempted—in one or two cases with considerable success—at some of the annual economic summits held over the past decade. At the same time there is scope for more economic cooperation on a regional basis, of the kind now being explored among the Pacific countries. The Lomé Convention linking the EEC with a group of African, Pacific and Caribbean countries could be built on in a number of valuable ways.

Economic coordination is by itself insufficient. It has to go wider and involve security issues and in the case of the trilateral countries grapple with the implications of defense expenditure and the political buttressing necessary for the preservation of a reasonable military balance with the Soviet Union. Yet security is not solely a military issue. There are other problems too, not least the maintenance of political stability—something that is itself strongly influenced by economic factors.

The early 1970s witnessed an upsurge of anxiety about the prospect of a rapid depletion of the world's limited stock of minerals and fossil fuels. This anxiety might seem to have been justified by the rise in oil prices over the subsequent decade—from around $2.50 a barrel in 1972 to $34 a barrel in 1982. But the fear of exhaustion of mineral resources soon came to be seen as misconceived, and even the dramatic increase in oil prices fell into perspective, as in large part a telescoping into a few years, as a result of the sudden consolidation of the power of OPEC, of increases in the real price of oil which should have taken place gradually over the previous two decades. Moreover, in the early 1980s, the twin forces of recession and energy conservation put severe downward pressure on real oil prices.

Nevertheless, the oil is beginning to run out. Within the next couple of decades it seems likely that oil production will have peaked and started to fall, and although natural gas production will go on rising for somewhat longer, the likelihood is that world energy demand will increasingly have to be met by coal and nuclear power. The very long lead-times involved, and the irreversibility of the build-up in the atmosphere of the carbon dioxide that results from the burning of fossil fuels, and of the danger represented by the increasingly widespread use of nuclear—particularly breeder—reactors make the question of a global strategy to develop inexhaustible energy sources such as solar power an increasingly urgent item on the international agenda. Haunting the necessary development of civil nuclear power is public concern over the building of such plants, and the reality of the increasing number of nuclear weapon-capable states despite the existence of the Non-Proliferation Treaty.

Other very serious environmental problems loom. By the year 2000, 40 per cent of the remaining forest cover in developing countries might disappear as a result of the desperate search of their inhabitants for fuelwood and more agricultural land. Such deforestation would lower the planet's ability to absorb carbon dioxide, reduce the quantity and quality of water supplies, and thereafter the genetic base of many of the world's crops and livestock. Another problem is a loss of cropland and degradation of the soil which may destroy more than a third of the world's arable land within the next twenty years. Another is the visible destruction of forests, and the damage done to lakes and rivers, by acid rain.

Problems such as these are not yet in the forefront of the consciousness of voters in the trilateral countries, and are consequently in grave danger of being neglected by politicians until it is too late. Yet they represent a set of trends of which a responsible political agenda for the trilateral countries must take urgent account in the choice of social, economic, political and strategic priorities to make democratic government work both efficiently and humanely in the decades ahead.

The history of the summit process involving discussion amongst heads of government is worth recalling in order to chart a strategy for the future. Early in 1973 the finance ministers of the United States, Britain, France and Germany, the so-called "Library Group," began to meet informally to discuss economic problems. Evolving from this the first summit of these four countries, Japan, and Italy took place in Rambouillet in November 1975. Summits have been held every year since, with the Prime Minister of Canada attending from 1977 and the President of the European Commission from 1978.

The utility of the summit process is difficult to assess. There is the usual problem of not knowing what would have happened in the absence of summits. Nevertheless there do appear to have been some achievements. One can perhaps distinguish between the achievements of the summit process as a whole, and the achievements of particular summits.

On the former, there is widespread agreement, for example, that the regular restatement of the May 1974 OECD pledge to maintain free trade has been a factor in holding protectionism at bay. The limited nature of the import controls imposed by the British Government in December 1975 has been attributed to the Rambouillet summit the previous month; the London summit of May 1977 seems to have given a crucial impetus to the Tokyo round of multilateral trade negotiations; and the approach of the Bonn summit in July 1978 helped again to overcome protectionist sentiment. In short, summitry has succeeded in helping the West hold the line on protectionism.

On the achievements of particular summits, the July 1978 Bonn summit was the most ambitious. Most of the participants pledged themselves to take action they probably would not otherwise have taken provided that the others did the same. This is described in more detail in Chapter V, *Tasks and Trade-Offs*. Various people, depending on their economic philosophy and political position, tend to ascribe success or failure to Bonn. But if the oil price rise of 1979 had not occurred it is possible to argue that the Bonn decisions would have averted the economic depression of 1980-82. What Bonn did above all was to demonstrate that only in a climate of political trade-offs can the summit process produce coordinated action.

Some other summits—such as the San Juan (Puerto Rico) summit of June 1976, and perhaps the Venice summit of June 1980—are generally reckoned to have achieved very little, though Venice, like the Tokyo summit the year before, did make a contribution to oil conservation policy. Others are less easy to evaluate. The 1977 London summit was important for starting to resolve U.S. anxieties over nuclear reprocessing and non-proliferation priorities and the French and German resentment at U.S. interference with their own decisions over their civil nuclear power programs. The Ottawa summit of July 1981 tends to be regarded as a failure; but it did permit a free discussion among the participants about the pros and cons of each other's policies, and particularly what were sometimes seen as the long-term benefits but short-term costs of American anti-inflationary policies. Even the Versailles summit of June 1982, usually regarded as little short of a disaster, seems to have had one important result: the communiqué called for a process of multilateral surveillance of exchange rates in cooperation with the IMF by the five countries—Britain, France, Germany, Japan and the United States, the Versailles Group—whose currencies determine the value of the Special Drawing Right (SDR). A number of informal meetings of the finance ministers of this Group of Five, and the Managing Director of the IMF, have been held since. The importance of these meetings— whose continuation was endorsed at Williamsburg—could be considerable. The importance of the Williamsburg summit of May 1983 was that for the first time the seven countries endorsed a mutual strategic objective, namely the need to respond to the Soviet missile program, and particularly the SS-20 deployment.

Unfortunately, there is a negative side to summits as well: they are becoming more like events devised for the media. Nevertheless, they do ensure a series of private and informal discussions among the heads of government on their own, for which they all have to be fully briefed. The benefits of such discussions, and the briefings of heads of government which lie behind them, may be difficult to identify, but real enough nonetheless.

Different people have different conceptions of how summits ought to work. Two particular views can be clearly distinguished. One is that summits should be occasions when a few heads of government discuss problems informally, with few if any aides present, and with a minimum of preparation and documentation on the part of their national bureaucracies. Moreover, such meetings should not necessarily be held regularly, but only when particularly important problems have arisen which might be resolved by such discussion.

The other view is that summits should represent the culmination of intensive discussions and negotiations both within and between government machines. Leaders should sign a pre-negotiated communiqué which sets the seal on months of hard bargaining on a variety of issues.

There are also different conceptions of how summits actually have worked. One view is that they have turned out to be a mixture of these two basic concepts. Another view is that the history of the summit process has displayed a kind of entropy: there has been a transition from candid and informal discussions, through institutionalized bureaucratic negotiations, to media occasions aimed mainly at the television cameras; the implication is that this degeneration is inevitable. A third, and even less favorable, view is that because attitudes to economic policy-making differ so widely among countries, the main value of summits lies in their public relations or confidence effects; and that nothing much more can be expected of them.

We believe that one can only develop a coordinated program if plans are laid for two or three summits in sequence and that such a building block approach has the best chance of achieving success. In that building process there is a place both for the informal spontaneous exchange and the more formal preplanned agreements. Diary problems alone make it inevitable that dates are fixed well in advance and we see no alternative to retaining a fixed annual cycle.

We are convinced that the necessity for strategic leadership in the world requires that the summits of the seven trilateral countries develop urgently the political dynamism and action orientation that they have hitherto lacked. Economic problems should not be discussed at heads of government level in isolation from other, often interrelated, political, military and strategic concerns. By restricting the agenda of the trilateral summits to economics there has been a considerable limitation on the scope for trading off individual countries' policy options across a wider agenda. Thus security issues should be of critical importance in planning future agendas.

In the rest of this report we discuss the main issues in more detail. Chapter II deals with *Employment and Equity*, Chapter III with *Interdependence and Growth*, and Chapter IV with *Cooperation or Fragmentation*. Finally, in Chapter V, we focus on the essential *Tasks and Trade-Offs* which the summit process should address to make democracy work.

II. EMPLOYMENT AND EQUITY: THE SOCIAL RESPONSE

Two central issues which confront our societies are addressed in this chapter: unemployment and the financing of social services. We begin with an analysis of three trends which are interwoven with these central issues. The first of these are demographic trends, of direct relevance to the problems both of unemployment and the financing of social services. Second is the microelectronic revolution, which is having profound effects on employment opportunities. Third is the rising share of government spending in national income. We then tackle the central issues directly, discussing ways in which they might be dealt with. A critical requirement for the resolution of both sets of problems—the resumption of faster economic growth—is a theme taken up in the following chapter.

TRENDS

DEMOGRAPHY

In the trilateral countries, there are two demographic trends of paramount importance. First, the post-war baby boom was followed virtually everywhere by a marked decline in the birth rate. In North America, this decline dates from the late 1950s, in Europe from the early 1960s. In Japan there was a very steep decline in the birth rate during the first half of the 1950s, followed by a further decline since the early 1970s. One effect of this has been—and will continue to be—a marked slowing-down in the growth of total population. Another has been a rise in the proportion of the population which is of working age, as those born during the baby boom have moved into the labor force. This factor should have had a favorable effect on growth rates and living standards, particularly since those in the 15-24 age group are more willing and able than older workers to move into sectors and areas where the demand for labor is rising. Unfortunately, the relatively slow growth in the demand for labor since the mid-1970s has largely dissipated this asset, though to varying degrees in the different trilateral regions. By and large it is not employment among the young, but unemployment, which has risen.

The second key demographic trend is that the population of the trilateral countries is an ageing population. Between 1960 and 1980 the proportion of the European population aged 65 and over rose from 10.5 per cent to 13.5 per cent, though for the time being the rise has levelled off. The proportion in North America rose from about 9 per cent to about 10.5 per cent over the same period, and is continuing to rise. In Japan the proportion of the population aged 65 and over was the lowest among the trilateral countries in 1960—about 6 per cent—but rose rapidly to almost 9 per cent in 1980. This rapid rise will continue: by the end of the century the proportion of the Japanese population in this age group is expected to have reached about 15 per cent, considerably higher than in North America. A particular problem is posed by the very old—those aged 80 and over—since the proper care of this age group is very expensive in terms of medical treatment and residential accommodation. The number of people in this category in the OECD countries as a whole grew from 12 million in 1970 to nearly 16 million in 1980, and is expected to be little short of 21 million by 1990.

MICROELECTRONICS

A second significant type of trend at work in the trilateral countries is the rapid and widespread adoption of microelectronic technology, which has profound implications for employment. Although in one sense this is merely the latest installment in the kind of technological change that has been at work raising productivity and living standards over the past two centuries, it is in other ways very different. One factor which is different is the speed with which the new technology has been developed and disseminated. The first integrated circuit was produced for military purposes in 1958, but it was only in the late 1960s that price falls led to a significant spread of the technology beyond the military field. The microprocessor—or central processing unit of a computer, contained on a chip—was first developed only in 1971. Yet by the end of the 1970s microelectronic technology had created new products and led to new techniques of production on a significant scale—a process which is rapidly continuing. Moreover, the technology itself is changing at breakneck speed: late in 1983, for example, one firm launched a new microprocessor chip which is said to be able to compute at 10 million instructions a second—as fast as the largest IBM computer of only three years earlier.

The microelectronic revolution has yielded, and will continue to yield, enormous benefits. One benefit is represented by new products,

ranging from consumer goods like video tape-recorders, pocket cal-
culators and electronic watches to services of various kinds, such as
electronic transfers of funds and mass air travel. Another benefit is new
processes of production which permit goods to be produced very
much more cheaply. More output, permitting higher consumption of
new and better goods, produced with less labor—this can reasonably
be regarded as constituting the kind of rise in living standards which is
the ultimate objective of economic policy. But there is another side to
the coin: the speed and scale of the microelectronic revolution has
begun to involve a significant displacement of labor. People who lose
their jobs—or fail to find them in the first place—because a computer
or robot can do the job better may find it easier to see the costs of the
process than the benefits.

Displacement of labor has been taking place particularly in manufacturing industry as, for example, robots replace men in car assembly
plants; and in the tertiary sector as, for example, the operations of
banks and insurance companies have become increasingly com-
puterized, reducing the need for certain types of clerical labor. Some of
the new products have a treble effect in displacing labor: electronic
typewriters or word processors are much cheaper to produce than
electro-mechanical typewriters, because they contain fewer components to manufacture and assemble; they significantly increase the
productivity of secretaries and typists; and, having few moving parts,
need less repair and maintenance. In consequence, the demand for
three different kinds of labor has been reduced by their introduction.

The reduction in the demand for many kinds of labor is, of course,
only part of the picture: there is rising demand for other kinds of labor.
In some cases one type of skilled labor is replaced by another: for
example, the linkages being established between numerically-controlled machine tools and computer-aided design reduce the demand for
draftsmen, precision engineers and toolsetters, but increase the demand for systems analysts and computer programmers. But in the
typical case it is semi-skilled and unskilled labor which is displaced by
the new technologies; the jobs created require skills and qualifications.

The overall effect that microelectronics will have on employment and
unemployment over the next decade or so is a matter of dispute. Some
of the studies which have been conducted come to the pessimistic
conclusion that the job losses which occur will not be compensated by
much employment creation elsewhere. The majority of studies are
more optimistic, concluding that compensation will be somewhere
between 50 and 100 per cent; and a few take the view that it may be over

100 per cent. For present purposes, however, there are two specific views which are of particular importance.

The first is the virtually unanimous belief among those who have studied the matter that far more jobs will be lost by countries which lag behind in the introduction of the new microelectronic technologies than by those which are in the vanguard of this process: indeed much of the difference in the estimates of compensation referred to above derives from different assumptions about the relative pace of introduction of these technologies in particular countries.

The second view, widely held in all three trilateral regions, is that Europe is already beginning to lag badly behind the United States and Japan in the speed and scale of its adjustment to the microelectronic era. But this is an oversimplified way of depicting the real situation. Although containing certain aspects of truth, such an assessment hides a far more complex state of affairs. There are certain sectors in which Europe as a whole is in the forefront of technical advance. These include nuclear energy and all the technologies connected with the nuclear fuel cycle; biotechnology, especially where the food and pharmaceutical industries are involved; even robotics and numerically-controlled machines, mainly where high precision or high flexibility instrumentation is required; and professional electronics, especially when applied to the public service sector including postal delivery, transportation and telecommunication systems. The other area of European strength is a proven ability to inject emerging technologies, such as lasers and microprocessors, into traditional industrial fields. This integration of new technologies and traditional sectors has allowed the revamping and rationalization of mature industries which only a few years ago seemed condemned to migrate to the Third World.

The relative weakness of Europe compared to the United States and to Japan is due to its low standing in a variety of solid state technologies: Very Large Scale Integrated Circuits and semi-conductors—such as the 'silicon chip'—advanced electronic components and circuits, and the development of large-scale computers, are not areas where Europe has been able to compete. This is an ominous trend for Europe and clearly much must be done if the problem—in these sectors at least—is not to continue to worsen.

The effects of the new microelectronic technology have been building up for little more than a decade, but they have been building up fast, and perhaps at an accelerating pace. Some of their impact on people's lives, both as producers and consumers, has already been felt, but much more is still to come. Handled properly, the new technology can confer great benefits not only on the trilateral countries where it has mainly been developed and adopted, but on the world as a whole. But there can be no confidence as yet that the large-scale displacement of labor that the new technology is bringing in its train can be successfully turned into greater leisure for all rather than permanent enforced idleness for those who are directly affected.

GOVERNMENT SPENDING

A third crucial trend over the last couple of decades has been a considerable growth in the role of the state in the economy of the trilateral countries, as reflected in the share of total general government expenditure in the national income (GDP or GNP). OECD statistics show that for the seven main trilateral countries taken together, this share rose from 28.7 per cent in 1960 to 32.6 per cent in 1970 and 40.6 per cent in 1982—a rise of 41 per cent over the whole 22 year period. For the United States and Japan, the shares in 1982 were virtually identical, at about 35.5 per cent; but for the United States this represented a rise of only 28 per cent from the 1960 figure of 27.8 per cent, whereas for Japan it represented a rise of 92 per cent, from a 1960 figure of only 18.3 per cent. In the four big European countries, the 1982 share ranged from 46.5 per cent in Britain to 54 per cent in Italy. For Italy, this represented a 79 per cent increase since 1960; for Britain, France and Germany the rise was in the range of 47-51 per cent. In Canada the 1982 figure was 46.4 per cent—a 61 per cent rise since 1960. The broad picture, then, is that in the United States and Japan the government is spending a little over a third of the national income, while in Europe and Canada the figure is closer to half. The increase in this ratio has been slow in the United States, fast in Japan, and somewhere in between in Europe and Canada.

A number of factors underlie this rising trend in the share of the national income spent by the government. One is the fact that as societies grow wealthier, they demand more services of a kind (such as better highways or cleaner air) that can often only be provided by state action. Another factor has been the ageing of the population: as the proportion of the population over 65 or over 80 rises, state retirement pensions necessarily rise, as does government expenditure—where government finances them—on the personal social services, residential homes and geriatric wards required by the elderly. A third factor in the rise in public expenditure as a share of the national income is the so-called "relative price effect": because the scope for raising productivity in many parts of the public sector is quite limited, the price of public sector output rises, at any given inflation rate, relative to the price of private sector output, and this will result in a rising ratio of public expenditure at current prices even if in real terms the share of the public sector remains the same.

A fourth factor is of more recent origin and, it is to be hoped, of less permanent duration. Rising unemployment has increased government expenditure on social security benefits, particularly in Europe, while in some recent years real GDP has been stagnant or falling. The effect of each factor has been to raise the share of the national income devoted to public expenditure.

Whatever the precise mixture of reasons in each trilateral region for the rapid growth in public expenditure over the past couple of decades, one consequence has been a rise in the burden of taxation. In Europe total tax revenue as a percentage of GDP rose from 27.8 per cent in 1965 to 34.4 per cent in 1975 and 37.5 per cent in 1981. In Canada it rose at much the same rate from 25.9 per cent of GDP in 1965 to 32.9 per cent in 1975 and 34.7 per cent in 1981. In the United States the rise was considerably slower—from 26.5 per cent in 1965 to 30.2 per cent in 1975 and 31.2 per cent in 1981. In Japan, on the other hand, it was considerably faster: it rose from only 17.8 per cent in 1965 to 21 per cent in 1975 and 26.9 per cent in 1981.

The widespread view that high taxes were inhibiting investment and growth has led in the last few years to vigorous efforts by most trilateral governments to cut back public expenditure. But the underlying factors making for rising public expenditure are powerful and pervasive: they consist not only of the demographic trends noted earlier, but also of such factors as rapidly rising American defense expenditure and a high level of agricultural and industrial subsidies in Europe. If it is deemed important to slow down or even halt the rising share of national income taken by public expenditure—and there are many conflicting views—hard choices in terms of electoral support will have to be made.

ISSUES

UNEMPLOYMENT

The Rise in Unemployment
The most serious social problem facing the trilateral countries at the present time is the level of unemployment. The OECD unemployment rate was 3 per cent in 1970. It rose to a little over 5 per cent in the mid-1970s in the wake of the first oil shock, and then stabilized. But

since the beginning of 1980 it has climbed dramatically. By late 1983 it was around 9 per cent, and still rising, albeit more slowly. In 1984 the rate may be around 10 per cent, representing some 35 million people.

Experience in the three trilateral regions has differed. In North America unemployment peaked at about 8.5 per cent in 1975, fell to around 6 per cent in 1979, and then rose sharply. But it peaked again, at about 11 per cent , at the end of 1982, and since then has been falling. In Western Europe, by contrast, there was no fall in unemployment during the mid-1970s, and the renewed rise since early 1980, which has brought it to over 10 per cent, shows no signs of going into reverse. In Japan, unemployment remains very low by the standards of its tri-lateral partners—though this partly reflects different techniques of measurement; even so, at around 2.5 to 3 per cent, it is twice as high as a decade ago.

Different groups have been affected differently by the rise in unem-ployment. Male unemployment has risen much faster than female unemployment since 1980, reflecting in some cases a slowing down in the growth of the female labor force, and the particularly severe effect of the recession on the mining, manufacturing and construction sec-tors, where male employment is high relative to female employment. Young people have been hit particularly hard. In the trilateral countries as a whole nearly one in five of those under 25 is without a job. In Japan the figure is relatively low—though still, at around 5 per cent, nearly twice the national unemployment rate. In the United States the figure is about 17 per cent, though among disadvantaged groups, particularly young blacks and Hispanics in the big cities, the figures are far higher. In a number of Western European countries the youth unemployment rate is well over 20 per cent, with much higher figures among ethnic minorities in particular areas. A further feature of the present unem-ployment problem is the rise in long-term unemployment, particularly in Western Europe, where more than a third of those who are unem-ployed have been unemployed for a year or more.

Causes of the Rise in Unemployment

Some observers have seen in the sharp rise in unemployment in recent years the operation of deep-seated and elusive forces at work in the world economy, as captured by the Kondratieff or long-wave theory of 50 year cycles of economic development: the deep recessions of the 1880s, the 1930s and now the 1980s, they argue, exhibit too great a regularity to be accidental. But no satisfactory explanation of why there should be such a regularity has been advanced, and the fact that only three observations of the phenomenon so far exist must make the data statistically suspect. Much more concrete explanations of the recent rise in unemployment can be pointed to.

One of these is the fact that, particularly since the mid-1970s, the population of working age in the trilateral countries has been rising faster than total population. The relationship between this phenomenon and the rise in unemployment is a complex one. In the EEC, where the labor force grew relatively slowly, unemployment grew fastest because there was an actual fall of 3 million in total employment between 1973 and 1983. In the United States, by contrast, a rapidly growing labor force and a marked rise in female participation rates were accompanied by the creation of 13 million new jobs over the same period. Nevertheless, a rise in the proportion of the population which is of working age, a demographic feature which would have helped to raise living standards if the demand for labor had been high, has contributed to swelling the ranks of the unemployed in the OECD as a whole at a time when the demand for labor has been low.

A much more significant factor behind the rise in unemployment, particularly in Western Europe, has been structural shifts in the demand for labor. Some of this has reflected the microelectronic revolution discussed earlier, and the significant savings of labor which the widespread adoption of the microprocessor is making possible in many manufacturing and service industries. But much of it reflects the more old-fashioned phenomenon of changing comparative advantage: not only Japan, but many of the newly industrializing countries as well, have become more efficient than Western Europe and part of North America at producing goods— textiles, clothing, footwear, steel, ships and a number of other products—which until relatively recently have constituted the bedrock output of the older industrial areas. In general, again particularly in Western Europe, resources have been slow to move out of these old industries into new ones; and although rising demand for both public and private services has led to an expansion of employment in the services sector, much of this extra employment has been provided by women not previously in the labor force, and has thus failed to lead to a corresponding fall in unemployment.

The second major reason for the sharp rise in unemployment in recent years lies in the macroeconomic policies which the trilateral countries have been pursuing. The rise in the inflation rate in the late 1960s and early 1970s, the further boost to world inflation given by the first oil shock of 1973-74, the plunge into balance of payments deficits of most of the main trilateral countries, and the fear of further inflationary and balance of payments problems after the second shock in 1979-80, all combined to promote restrictive macroeconomic policies in these countries, particularly after 1979. These policies have been successful in the sense that the OECD inflation rate has been brought down from around 12 per cent in 1980 to 6 per cent in 1983, and to an even lower rate in most of the main trilateral countries. But the other side of the coin was that between 1979 and 1983 total OECD output grew, on average, by little more than 1 per cent a year—much more slowly than the underlying growth in productivity. The resulting fall in the demand for labor has obviously been a prime factor in the rise in unemployment.

The Damage of High Unemployment

A high rate of unemployment which represents short spells out of work for a large number of people is not necessarily to be deplored: it may be a reflection of a society adapting rapidly to change. But the contemporary phenomenon— particularly in Western Europe—of a high rate of unemployment which represents prolonged periods of joblessness for a minority of the labor force, is particularly damaging. It conflicts with the work ethic which underlies the growth in prosperity in the trilateral countries over the past century, according to which able-bodied citizens must contribute to the creation of this prosperity if they are to enjoy its fruits. For those who suffer involuntary unemployment, such a contribution is rendered impossible, and the basis on which society is organized is correspondingly weakened. The marked increases in labor productivity being made possible by the micro-electronic revolution call, over the next decade, for some new thinking about the relationships between work, income and leisure. The hallmark of democratic governments worldwide cannot be a fatalistic acceptance of the permanent unemployment of a large and possibly growing proportion of their labor force.

Two of the groups which suffer from long-term unemployment are particular objects of concern. One is the middle-aged—particularly men—who lose their jobs because their firm closes down or their skills are made obsolete by technical progress. Some of these people take advantage of their enforced leisure, developing new skills and interests, but others suffer a loss of self-respect, become apathetic or depressed, and lose interest in life. Even more serious is the plight of the other group—the youthful unemployed. Young people who on leaving school or after higher education search in vain for a job for months which can stretch into years are likely to feel—and with some justice—that they have been rejected by society. That some of them should take refuge in alcohol, drugs or crime is hardly surprising; but it is a searing indictment of the failure of the societies in which they have grown up to provide them with a fundamental human right: the right to work. It is no use extolling the merits of democracy on the one hand while on the other ignoring this social evil that has once again, as in the 1920s and '30s, returned to dwell on the conscience of the democracies.

Undue alarmism may well be out of place; but so is undue complacency. It does not seem particularly fanciful to discern, in high rates of long-term unemployment among the young, the seeds of a threat to our democratic system. This is particularly true of Western Europe, where youth unemployment rates of well over 20 per cent are already common, and where, on present trends, the problem is going to get worse. On the other side of the ideological divide, in Eastern Europe, there appears, by contrast, to be no great unemployment problem. It is easy for well-informed observers to point to the gross inefficiencies and high level of disguised unemployment in the Soviet system, and to argue that one of the Soviet Union's methods of preventing overt unemployment is to force millions of people to work in uncongenial jobs and in unpleasant places like Siberia. But to a generation of young people in Western Europe facing the prospect of an indefinite period of unemployment and a standard of living no higher than that provided by social security benefits, the relative attractions of the democratic and communist systems could come to assume a different perspective. Already, the claim that parliamentary democracy is incapable of solving our economic and social problems is increasingly being heard in Europe. Nor can we in the industrialized democracies dismiss unemployment or perennial underemployment in the developing world. Here too, its recent rapid growth, admittedly from a higher initial base, gives grounds for concern. Many of these countries—including such democratic countries as India—favor some form of non-alignment, preferring not to choose between the ideologies of communism or capitalism; but even the choice of non-alignment is not fixed. The Soviets certainly pursue in these countries their version of the "ideological struggle" and we in the trilateral countries cannot be indifferent to any ideological shift towards communism particularly where it carries with it security implications.

FINANCING SOCIAL SERVICES

In an attempt to minimize the political implications of unemployment it is sometimes argued that one cannot compare our current problems with the 1920s and 1930s because our democratic societies have now accepted the obligation of providing a system of social security which shields everyone from the stark poverty experienced in past recessions. In large part in consequence of shouldering this obligation, public expenditure, as a proportion of the national income, has been rising in all the trilateral countries for the past twenty years or more. In the United States and Japan, the ratio is now over a third; in Western Europe and Canada it is closer to half. However justified the reasons for these increases may be, the fact remains that public expenditure on this scale can only be financed by a combination of taxation and government borrowing that can have adverse effects on the operation of market economies. High taxes can inhibit saving and investment, and discourage the innovation, risk-taking and entrepreneurial drive which underlie economic progress and increasing prosperity. High levels of government borrowing can lead to either high interest rates, which may crowd out productive private sector investment, or to increases in the money supply which may fuel inflation.

These dangers have been increasingly recognized by trilateral governments in recent years and attempts have been made to cut back public expenditure as a share of the national income. So far, little success has been achieved. Part of the reason for this lies in a "can't win" situation: cuts in public expenditure which, in the short run at any rate, result in people becoming unemployed instead of moving into the private sector of the economy, depress the national income while at the same time adding to state payments of social security benefits. But there are deeper reasons than this. The hard choices that must be made are often electorally unpopular and are, therefore, not being made. Agricultural and industrial subsidies which should have been phased out years ago are still being paid. Declining industries which should have been allowed to die are being kept alive. Social security benefits which should have been concentrated on those in need often go to the better-off. Though the nature of the choices may differ somewhat in the different trilateral regions, we are all tending to suffer because of the interrelated nature of our economies.

In the United States, taxes have been cut, particularly for the higher income groups; social security payments have risen rapidly, as have interest payments on the national debt; and very large increases in defense expenditure have been undertaken. The consequence at present is a budget deficit of some $200 billion, equivalent to over 5 per cent of the GNP. The increase in the deficit over the last few years has in one way been welcome: it has provided the United States with a Keynesian-type fiscal stimulus which has led to a rapid revival of the economy and, by raising American imports, contributed to expansion in other countries as well. However, in this situation the combination of a low American propensity to save and a tight control of the growth of the money supply has meant very high real interest rates not only in the

United States itself, where the costs to borrowers have until very recently been muted by a comprehensive system of tax relief on interest payments, but around the world. In the interests of both the American economy and the global economy the budget deficit must now be quickly and substantially reduced: either the rapid growth of U.S. defense expenditure must be cut back through its burden being more equally shared across the trilateral countries or as a result of negotiated conventional and nuclear arms reductions which would not endanger the security of the West; or U.S. non-defense expenditure must be cut back; or taxation levels must be increased. Indeed this is probably an understatement: many observers take the view that the scale of the problem is such that action on all three fronts is needed as a matter of urgency.

In Europe, the situation is not very different. The rapidly rising prosperity which occurred during the 25 years after the immediate post-war recovery permitted the creation of an ambitious nexus of social services sometimes known as "the welfare state". To a high degree, European countries provide free or subsidized health and educational services and generous benefits for retired people, the unemployed and sick, and disadvantaged groups of other kinds. Demographic factors—notably the increasing proportion of the population which is old or very old— have made these provisions increasingly expensive, as has the recent high level of unemployment; and the problem has been exacerbated by a relatively high level of subsidies to agriculture and to declining industries such as textiles, steel and shipbuilding. The financing of these expenditures out of taxation and employers' and employees' social security contributions feasible in a buoyant rapidly growing economy has been progressively harder to accomplish as growth has slowed and the recession has contributed to an inward looking and less generous mood. This financial burden may well have had significant adverse effects on incentives, competitiveness, investment and growth, and thus be in part responsible for the relative decline of the European economy.

In Japan, some of these problems lie in the future rather than the present—but the future is drawing very near. Increasing pressures are likely to be felt for improved social security arrangements, and demographic changes are not on Japan's side. As was indicated earlier, between 1980 and 2000 the proportion of the population aged 65 and over will rise rapidly, from around 9 per cent to around 15 per cent, and this will correspondingly increase the cost not only of retirement pensions, but also of medical services for the elderly.

Whatever the precise differences in the situation in which different trilateral countries find themselves, the underlying dilemma is the same. How, in an era in which economic growth may be slower than in the past, and faced in varying degrees by ageing populations, can they provide acceptable levels of social services to those unable to provide for themselves, while at the same time creating or preserving a market system of rewards and incentives which will promote the innovation and dynamism upon which economic progress must be founded?

POLICIES

TACKLING THE UNEMPLOYMENT PROBLEM

Our view is that the problem of high unemployment must be tackled simultaneously at three different levels. We discuss each of these approaches in turn.

Sustained Economic Growth

A crucial feature of any program for reducing the level of unemployment in the trilateral countries must be the resumption of a faster rate of economic growth than has been achieved in recent years. Effective demand must be expanded more rapidly, and methods of dealing with inflation must be devised which do not rely on the kind of restrictive fiscal and monetary policies which have been the norm in most of the trilateral countries in recent years.

The problem of achieving economic growth is discussed in Chapter III, and in this chapter we do no more than emphasize one aspect of the problem which is of particular relevance to the social response our countries must make to the unemployment problem. The types of effective demand which will need to be expanded will include not only demand for the goods and services which will be produced so abundantly as a result of the microelectronic revolution, but also for the kind of services produced in sectors in which labor productivity will be much more difficult to increase. Some of these services—such as health, educational and environmental services—are often provided by the public sector, particularly in Europe, and their expansion, while providing considerable scope for extra employment, will impinge on the other crucial issue discussed in this chapter, the problem of financing social services.

Active Labor Market Policies

Increasing effective demand will not, by itself, be nearly enough; active measures will need to be taken, on a widespread and sustained basis, to ensure that the labor force has the required skills to meet the demand, and is available at the right place and the right time.

The role of the government in this process is likely to differ in the different trilateral regions. In the United States there is a long tradition of a high degree of labor mobility, in two different senses. Workers have shown considerable willingness to acquire new skills and qualifications, in order to better themselves and increase their earning power. The geographical mobility of American families—the readiness to move long distances to new locations as seen in the drift to the South and Southwest in the pursuit of a better job—is of an order quite unfamiliar in Europe where there is an expectation—not in itself unreasonable, but sometimes over-pitched—that governments will bring jobs to deprived regions. American trade unions, moreover, have traditionally welcomed and contributed to the process of technological change, taking the view that this process is the key to higher living standards, at any rate for those who manage to adapt to these changes and to keep their jobs.

An encouraging trend, widespread throughout the trilateral regions, is the shift to service industries. Part of the natural evolution of Western industrial societies, it offers scope for absorbing large numbers of unemployed. In the United States, for example, nearly all the increase of 13 million jobs between 1973 and 1983 was in three main service areas: wholesale and retail trading; finance, insurance and real estate; and professional, scientific and miscellaneous services. Compared to some European countries, especially Britain, a much higher proportion of the increase in the demand for services fed straight through into an increase in employment.

Japan, like the United States, has a tradition—albeit a more recent one —of a workforce ready to adapt to changing patterns of demand. Under the system of lifetime employment prevalent in the bigger companies, employees agree to be trained and re-trained for new jobs, and moved from one location to another, in return for the guarantee of continued employment. The result, as in America, is a workforce instinctively inclined to welcome rather than resist technological change; though even in Japan the lifetime employment system only applies to a minority of employees; and there are temporary workers who lose their jobs at a time of declining demand.

The position in Europe is, in important respects, different. For whatever complex of reasons—its older industrial tradition, its larger trade union membership, the pervasive sense of a society with its roots still deep in the past, or attitudes inbred by the physical destruction wrought by two world wars fought over its soil within the lifetime of its older inhabitants— the resistance to change is greater. By comparison with the United States and Japan, labor markets are relatively inflexible. Workers are less willing to accept technological change, less willing to be re-trained for new jobs, and less willing to move in search of employment. The degree of inflexibility does indeed vary substantially within Europe—it is considerably greater in Britain than in Germany, for example—but by and large it presents a greater problem than in other trilateral regions. There is in Europe a tendency for governments to provide subsidies to keep older and increasingly uncompetitive industries in business, rather than to use the money to alleviate the costs of adaptation to the changing pattern of comparative advantage. This process is justified on the basis that it is better to have people producing goods which are strictly uncompetitive in world markets than to have people producing nothing at all. But too often assistance which is devised in order to cushion the process of change in the short term becomes institutionalized into a system of subsidies in the long term; and the result of this can only be an increasingly arthritic industrial structure, increasingly unable to adapt to new developments or to pay its way in a rapidly changing world.

One suggestion which has been discussed in Europe to improve the workings of the labor market is to cut the level of unemployment benefits, on the supposition that many people find it more agreeable to live on state benefits than to work. But surveys in a number of European countries suggest that this is no more than a marginal problem, and that by far the greatest part of unemployment is genuinely involuntary. Increasingly therefore solutions are being sought in ways of making labor markets more flexible, encouraging workers without skills, or with skills that have been rendered obsolete by technical progress, to be trained or re-trained. Although it will sometimes pay private employers to do this, the ultimate responsibility for stimulating the extensive training and re-training that is necessary will lie with the state. It is society as a whole that benefits from the higher living standards made possible by technical progress, and it is society as a whole—rather than the individuals directly affected—which must bear the costs of adapting to such change. More vocational training for the young, and a system of re-training for adults whose skills are overtaken by changing job requirements, must come to be regarded as essential obligations of government if the problem of structural unemployment is to be overcome.

New Thinking on Work and Leisure
The potential increases in productivity stemming from the microelectronic revolution pose the question of how far even sustained economic growth and active labor market policies will, by themselves, solve the unemployment problem if work continues to be governed by

present custom and practice in terms of the hours worked in a week, the weeks worked in a year, and the age of retirement. The fall in the number of young people entering the labor force over the next decade may alleviate the problem of youth unemployment, but is unlikely to solve it. What is needed now is some new thinking about the relationship between hours worked and leisure enjoyed. What must be avoided is a situation in which a majority of the population—though a shrinking one—works traditional hours for a traditional working lifetime, while a minority of the population—though an increasing one—does not work at all. Instead the aim should be to devise arrangements which offer some opportunity for work, and more opportunities for leisure, to all.

The elements of such arrangements are relatively easy to discern. One is likely to be a longer period of compulsory education or broad vocational training for the young—something in any case needed as part of a more active labor market policy. Another would be a shorter working week, or longer annual holidays, or some combination of the two. Another would be a general lowering of the age of retirement—though it must be recognized that in the United States, for example, there is some pressure from workers to raise rather than lower the retirement age. Another part of the answer may be a move towards more extensive job-sharing or part-time working. Important sections of the labor force, such as married women and older workers nearing retirement, are likely to welcome greater opportunities than are generally available at present to work on a part-time basis, rather than work full-time or not at all. The expansion of job opportunities in the service sector should in principle make this desire easier to satisfy. However, the fact that such elements of a solution as these may be relatively easy to discern does not necessarily mean that the solution will be simple to achieve. Two difficulties in particular must be faced.

The first is the danger that any major move towards work-sharing—i.e. more people at work, but most of them working shorter hours—may confront employers with a significant rise in unit costs; this problem may be especially acute where what is at issue is a shift to a shorter working week or longer paid annual holidays. A rise in unit costs can lead to an erosion of profit margins or an upward twist to inflation, and—if exchange rates are sticky—to a decline in international competitiveness. However, the risk of a significant rise in unit costs is sometimes exaggerated. The underlying rationale of the need to reduce working hours if a high level of employment is to be restored and maintained is that the microelectronic revolution makes possible a large increase in the amount produced per working hour, so that the increase in labor costs per hour— assuming that employees work fewer hours per year for the same money—may be offset or more than offset by rising productivity. Thus unit costs—costs per unit of output—may be stable or even falling. Of course it will not always be the case that the rise in productivity permitted by the chip and other technological developments will be sufficient to allow big reductions in working hours at unchanged—or even increased—wages. This is most obvious in the case of people who choose to move from full-time to part-time work, who would naturally not expect to earn the same amount of money: they have opted for less income and more leisure. Moreover, there is bound to be a continuing struggle over the distribution of the fruits of the higher productivity resulting from the microelectronic revolution between workers—who want more income for fewer hours, employers—who want higher profits, and consumers—who want lower prices. Thus it is desirable that the workers' share of rising prosperity should take the form not of rapidly rising income—but no increase in leisure—for some, but rather of a more modest rise in income, and some increase in leisure for all. Providing that the increase in leisure is matched to increasing productivity, there is no reason why these changes should result in any increase in inflationary pressures or—in an era of flexible exchange rates —in any reduction of international competitiveness.

A second difficulty that may arise in a strategy of encouraging work-sharing and increased leisure as part of the answer to high unemployment is that some of those who have secure jobs may insist on receiving more income rather than more leisure; in other words may be unwilling to cooperate in policies designed to share the available employment more equitably.

It is difficult to know how far this will really prove a problem. It is true that some groups of workers resist cuts in weekly hours of work— or, if hours are cut, resort to moonlighting rather than enjoy the extra leisure. But the same groups of workers often welcome longer annual holidays or earlier retirement, so that the effect of reduction in lifetime hours of work can be achieved by one route rather than another. The history of the past hundred years is one of higher living standards in the industrialized countries taking the form of both higher incomes and more leisure, and there is no particular reason why this pattern should change in the future.

Nevertheless, the sheer speed of contemporary technological change does raise the distinct possibility that the pace at which workers or employers may wish of their own accord to reduce lifetime hours of work may not be rapid enough to help provide job opportunities for the unemployed. If this is so, governments in the trilateral countries will have to take the lead—though the form this lead will take will obviously vary according to the nature of the problem in each country, and the attitude of its people. There is much that governments can do to encourage the process. Taxation and social security systems can be adjusted, for example, so as to make part-time employment more attractive to both employer and employee. The financial penalties resulting from early retirement can also be reduced by appropriate tax and benefit provisions. More specifically, where a firm agrees to replace an older worker by a young unemployed worker, the pension or redundancy payments incurred by the firm could in part be financed by the state, which would be saving on unemployment benefits to the younger worker.

However, although governments must give a lead, fostering a climate of opinion favorable to a shorter working lifetime and more leisure for all, and providing appropriate financial incentives and disincentives, the ultimate willingness to adapt to the needs of the microelectronic age must come from employers and employees themselves. Individuals must have a greater say in determining the way in which their working lives are organized. Our democracies must show themselves capable—as we are confident they will—of making the adjustments at the level of the local plant and the local community that will be needed if the benefits of the new technologies are to be spread fairly throughout our societies.

FINANCING SOCIAL SERVICES

As was indicated earlier, one of the crucial problems facing the trilateral countries is the question of how, particularly in an era in which some factors may be unfavorable to growth, the social services—in the wide sense of retirement pensions, unemployment and sickness benefits, together with the provision of health and educational services—are going to be financed. The issue is already critical in Europe, where a welfare state built up at a time when growth was fast and expectations optimistic is proving increasing difficult to finance even against a background of high taxes and social security contributions and sizeable budget deficits. In the United States, too, the problem is causing increasing alarm: although the relatively small means-tested benefits have been cut back hard—some would say too hard—the far larger body of non means-tested federal entitlements, which now account for 40 per cent of the entire federal budget, have hardly been touched. Because, for demographic reasons, they are received by a growing proportion of the population, because they are nearly all index-linked to prices, and because they include the rapidly escalating cost of medical treatment, they are currently growing at an annual rate of around 15 per cent—about twice as fast as money GNP. Even in Japan, where a rapidly ageing population means, for example, that by the year 2000 the number of old people receiving pensions will be four times as high as in 1980, the problem is beginning to loom large.

There is a real dilemma here which the trilateral countries need to consider together. Even if detailed solutions will inevitably tend to be reached separately, there is a mutual interest in trying to establish a global social-economic environment which helps rather than hinders the preservation of the essentials of a caring society. On the one hand, a system of social provision which to some extent insulates every family's standard of living—and in particular everyone's access to publicly-provided health and educational services—from the arbitrary ups and downs of life is a sign of a mature and civilized society, and worth considerable financial sacrifice to maintain. Demand for the provision of other "public goods" such as urban and environmental services which by their nature must be made available to all is notoriously difficult to assess, and may be considerably greater than is suggested by public opinion surveys which invite people to ask for lower taxes without making clear the consequences of such an option for the quality of life. If these public services can be provided efficiently, it is likely that most people would be willing to help finance them. On the other hand social security benefits, where cash payments are universal, are becoming a very high percentage of government expenditure. By definition these payments represent, at a macroeconomic level, transfers from those who are producing wealth to those who are not. The higher the level of benefits, and the larger the number of recipients in relation to the total population, the greater is the burden on the productive elements in society. Here the case for selectivity is becoming overwhelming, and the signs are that unless this political nettle is grasped the standards of provision of health, educational and environmental services will inevitably deteriorate.

This dilemma, which confronts all democracies with market-orientated systems of producing and distributing wealth, is clearly tied up with the problem of unemployment. The more successful our countries are in reducing unemployment, the smaller will be the deadweight cost of paying unemployment benefits. The larger the proportion of the population in some form of paid employment, the lower will be the society's need for state-funded social services and social security payments, and the greater its ability to finance those which are needed.

Nevertheless, although faster growth and lower unemployment will clearly be critical ingredients in any satisfactory solution of the problem, they will not be enough on their own. In our societies a balance must be struck between providing inadequate social services, with unacceptable poverty and deprivation, and providing over-generous social services, which are a disincentive to working for a living, and which impose a crushing burden on those whose entrepreneurship and work provide the dynamic of our market-orientated economies. In recent years the balance in our societies may have tilted too far in the latter direction mainly because of the pursuance of the universal ethos of welfare provision rather than the selective approach which if properly applied is capable of concentrating provision on those most in need. To redress this balance, there will have to be reductions in the provision of free or subsidized assistance to those who are capable of helping themselves, and greater channeling of the resources of the state more directly to those whose needs are greatest. There is also considerable scope for a greater degree of voluntary service to the community. In this way tasks and activities which contribute to the well-being of society can be undertaken by people who are retired or for some other reason are without paid employment. Such arrangements in turn bring benefits to those who provide voluntary service, involving them in worthwhile activities and giving them a sense of being needed by the community. At the same time, people must be encouraged to make greater provision for themselves against the contingencies of unemployment, sickness and old age. Governments can help significantly to achieve this aim, for example by gearing the tax system in ways that encourage earning and saving and discourage spending.

CONCLUSION

The implications of this chapter can be very briefly summarized. If the scourge of high unemployment is to be removed from our societies—as it must be, no less on political than on social and moral grounds—we shall need not only faster economic growth and more active labor market policies, but also new thinking about the relationship between work and leisure. People must be encouraged and helped to stay longer in full-time education and training; to retire earlier; to welcome the opportunity to work fewer hours per week or take longer annual holidays; or to take sabbaticals in the course of their working lives in order to re-train for new careers or simply to engage in private pursuits. In every case, the aim must be to help people see the greater leisure made possible by the advent of the microelectronic era as a gateway to the achievement of fuller and more satisfying lives.

Intertwined with this objective must be the aim of encouraging people to assume a greater measure of responsibility for insuring against the vicissitudes of life. The state can only provide assistance to some individuals if this assistance is paid for by others. In some of our societies, particularly perhaps in Western Europe, reliance on the state has gone too far, and the result has been a loss of drive and dynamism, and a playing-down of the importance of market forces as the progenitor of change and progress, which casts a shadow over the prospects of future prosperity. More must be done to hand back to our people themselves the responsibility for the decisions which will shape their destiny. The enabling state should be the objective for the next century: concerned and compassionate about those unable to help themselves, but more selective in choosing its priorities and roles, and more relaxed about the diversities that are part of a free society.

III. Interdependence and Growth: The Economic Response

The almost four decades since the end of the second world war have witnessed a tremendous acceleration of world economic development and integration. The war and early postwar conditions created a political and economic climate conducive to the establishment of international institutions and national economic policies that favored recovery, trade, capital liberalization and growth. From about the mid-1960s, however, conditions began to change. Inflation became an increasing problem, and the problem was exacerbated by the fact that inflation occurred at very different rates in different countries. Productivity, too, grew more rapidly in some countries than in others. The Bretton Woods international monetary system, based on fixed exchange rates pegged to the dollar, collapsed. Trade negotiations became more complex and difficult to organize as the number of important economies increased and after the more easily defined areas of concessions were exhausted. Moreover, national governments have found it increasingly hard to make the tremendous internal and international adjustments forced by rapid economic development and changing patterns of international competitiveness.

Since 1970, the world economy has lurched from crisis to crisis. There has been no systemic breakdown, nor have these crises made the Soviet economic system appear more attractive, since the Soviets' own economic problems have also been very much in evidence. However, confidence in the postwar economic institutions has been eroding among the trilateral publics and with it the value of international economic cooperation itself has come under question.

At the danger of over-simplification, one can distinguish three general categories of trilateral responses to the economic crises of the past several years. First, there are those who advocate a return to what they perceive as the more certain economic world of the past. Falling into this category, for example, are those who want a return to fixed exchange rates (or even the gold standard), those who advocate restrictions on the activities of multinational corporations, and those who advocate trade protection to preserve established national industries. An opposite kind of response is to advocate supranational economic institutions, such as a world central banking authority. The mainstream response, however, has been the patchwork repair or renovation of existing institutions. Most of the trilateral governments have responded to the economic crises of the 1970s and early 1980s in this manner.

We believe that a concerted effort to return to the past would restrict growth and be incompatible with world economic trends and with human aspirations. Fundamental changes have occurred which cannot be reversed except at the cost of extreme economic dislocation and human suffering. On the other hand, new worldwide institutions and authorities are not politically feasible or desirable at the present time. Yet simply "muddling through" is a dangerous and irresponsible course. Dealing with the economic challenges of the coming decade requires a longer term vision and consistent policies to make that vision a reality. While it can be argued that the political realities facing democratic governments make any course other than muddling through impractical, providing goals and realistic means of moving toward those goals are essential elements of creative political management.

In this chapter, we will set out in broad terms our view of the longer term changes in the world economy, the potential dangers if appropriate action is not taken, and our assessment of the important issues which the trilateral governments must address. In the concluding chapter we outline a series of important steps which could be implemented through the economic summit process over the next several years.

TRENDS IN THE WORLD ECONOMY

World Economic Integration
The integration of the world economy, often described by the term "interdependence", has been increasing at a rapid pace. The stage for this was set by the emergence of the United States as the world's predominant power after the war, and the constant pressure it exerted in favor of a free world trading system and freedom for international capital flows. Subsequently, growing interdependence was fostered by the fact that the two most dynamic economies between about the mid-1950s and the mid-1970s—Germany and Japan—enjoyed rapidly rising exports; by the growth of multinational corporations, with global sources of supply, production facilities, and markets; and by revolutionary changes in transport and communications. One measure of this rapid growth in interdependence has been the increase in world exports as a percentage of world GNP, from 12.6 per cent in 1970 to 21.2 per cent in 1980. Another is the huge rise in the volume of international

capital flows, particularly short and medium-term capital flows, especially over the past 15 years or so.

The reality of world economic integration has been most starkly demonstrated in the world petroleum trade. Trade in oil, worth about $450 billion a year, is far greater than trade in any other commodity, and the price of oil, more than any other single factor, was the cause of the crises and adjustments in the world economy over the past decade. The meteoric price rises in 1973-74 and 1979-80 triggered two recessions and forced the world industrial and financial systems to adjust to the massive changes in relative economic costs and power. Such shifts, for example, by increasing the demand for smaller cars, greatly strengthened the competitive strength of the Japanese versus the American automobile industry, but at the same time dealt severe blows to the high energy-consuming Japanese aluminum and petrochemical industries. More generally, the oil price increases resulted in the accelerated obsolescence of much industrial equipment, and dealt a great blow to most Third World states whose growth rates were dramatically cut. The recent oil price drop may, by contrast, result in delay in the development of new technology designed to conserve energy.

Slow-down of Growth in the Trilateral Economies

There has been a slow-down in growth rates since the early 1970s, especially in the trilateral world, which reflects in part the end of rapid recovery and growth in Japan and Western Europe and in part the economic recessions of the past decade. For the developed countries as a whole, GDP grew on average by 5 per cent a year in the 1960s and 3.2 per cent in the 1970s. Between 1980 and 1982 growth averaged less than 1 per cent a year, though the recovery from recession, particularly in the United States, will probably have raised the figure to about 3 per cent a year between 1982 and 1984.

It is difficult to distinguish between cycles and long-term trends, and growth in the 1980s may well be faster than it was in the troubled 1970s. But faster growth certainly cannot be taken for granted. There are at least five reasons why the growth of the GDP might be expected to be slower over the next decade. Two of these are essentially a consequence of national income accounting conventions, and should not be regarded as a cause of concern. First, output in many parts of the service sector is difficult to measure, and is often assumed to move in line with inputs, so that the figures show no increase in productivity. With an increasing proportion of the labor force being employed in the service sector, this is bound to have the statistical effect of slowing down the growth of the GDP. The same effect will result from the second factor—

a move towards shorter lifetime hours of work of the kind discussed in the previous chapter. A voluntary increase in leisure, at the expense of work and income, must increase people's welfare, or they would not choose it; but it reduces the GDP, which is a measure of output and not of human satisfaction.

Of the other three reasons why slower growth of the GDP may be expected, one reflects the fact that the removal of barriers to trade and capital flows which was such a stimulus to growth in the first few decades after the war—the creation of the European Economic Community being an obvious example—has largely come to an end. Non-tariff barriers remain a large and perhaps increasing problem; but there seems little prospect of their removal on a scale comparable to the reduction of tariffs which resulted from the successive post-war multi-lateral trade negotiations such as the Kennedy and Tokyo Rounds. A fourth reason for expecting slower growth lies in the slowing-down of the growth of productivity, particularly in the American economy, in recent years. Since there is no consensus on the reasons for this slow-down, no one can say whether it is a temporary phenomenon or a permanent one; but it would be unwise to discount it completely.

The fifth reason for expecting that growth may be slower over the next decade or so than it was in the 1950s and 1960s is the one that causes us much concern: macroeconomic policies. We believe that macroeconomic policies have an important impact on growth rates, and that policies which overlook this fact, and which focus almost exclusively on eliminating inflation or reducing public expenditure or the growth of the money supply, are likely to lead to slower growth rates than are either feasible or desirable. We return to the implications of this later on.

Changing Structure of World Economic Power
There have been two principal trends in the structure of world economic power over the past three decades: the relative (not absolute) decline in the position of the United States and the rapid advance of Japan, which is now being diffused more broadly across the economies of East Asia. The proportion of world GNP represented by East Asia—Japan, South Korea, Taiwan, Hong Kong, and the ASEAN countries—and Oceania—Australia, New Zealand and the South Pacific—expanded from 6.1 per cent in 1960 to 13.6 per cent in 1980. During the same two decades, the United States share declined from 33.4 per cent to 22.4 per cent. The general direction of these two trends is expected to be the same during the next two decades, though the rate of change is projected to be much smaller than in the past.

The consequence of these trends has been the establishment of a new center of world industrial and economic power in East Asia that is rapidly approaching in size the older centers in North America and Western Europe. This implies at least two general problems which have been highlighted in a previous task force report to the Trilateral Commission (*Sharing International Responsibilities Among the Trilateral Countries*, 1982). First, the regions with newly acquired economic power need to assume a financial and political commitment to the health, management, and security of the international system as a whole, and second, the older centers need to accept the new actors as essential components of the system and be willing to share with them the management of the system.

The shift in relative economic power should be kept in perspective. Although in recent years the relative position of North America and Western Europe has declined *vis-à-vis* Japan, both regions are continuing to advance, and the more rapid advance of Japan and the developing countries makes a net positive contribution to the growth of the older industrialized countries. The United States remains the world's largest single economic unit, and is relatively much less dependent on outside resources. The U.S. domination in capital markets and the role of the dollar remain disproportionately large compared to the size of the U.S. economy, and this means that U.S. domestic policy will continue to be very significant in the world economy. In this context, the current U.S. recovery and U.S. macroeconomic policy have important longer term global implications, a point to which we will return later.

Similarly, the relative European decline should not be exaggerated. The world's richest industrial economies in terms of per capita income—Switzerland and West Germany—are in Western Europe, and in aggregate the European GNP is about the same size as that of North America.

DANGERS OF THE COMING DECADE

Economic Collapse

The most extreme danger of the decade ahead, a major collapse of the world economic system, is also the least likely. One can distinguish between two potential causes of collapse. The first is a major shock, such as the actual default of a major debtor country, leading to a chain-reaction of defaults by other debtor countries, the consequences of which could not be immediately contained. Such a shock could be initiated either by economic forces or by political or military events, such as those associated with both the first and second oil shocks. So far, the world economic system has proved remarkably resilient, sustaining both oil shocks and appearing to surmount the continuing developing country debt crisis. However, responsible statesmanship seeks to minimize the dangers of sudden system-wide crisis, and hence the risk of this kind of breakdown.

The second kind of collapse could come not from a sudden shock, but from the more insidious effects of a series of irresponsible or dysfunctional policies, such as the competitive protectionist measures which various governments took in the early 1930s. The current protectionist climate in some of the major trilateral countries is certainly dangerous, because even if government leaders appreciate the need for maintenance of the open trade system, public pressures are forcing governments incrementally in protectionist directions. This danger makes it essential that trilateral governments have a well-articulated and positive strategy for managing the international economy.

The Continuation of Slow Growth

A much more likely danger is a fizzling out of the current economic recovery and relatively slow growth throughout the rest of the decade. As we have seen in the previous chapter, slow growth means that the serious socio-economic problems the trilateral countries are currently facing—such as high unemployment and difficulties of financing desired social services—become harder to overcome. By contrast, economic adjustments are easier to achieve in a rapidly growing economy where new job opportunities are continually opening up even as older industries are allowed to decline.

In a larger economic framework, slow growth in the trilateral countries has wide implications for the developing countries, and would make it impossible for the debtor countries to earn enough foreign exchange to continue servicing their external debt. Thus in the longer term, the slow growth danger becomes less and less distinguishable from the economic collapse scenario because slow growth weakens support for international economic institutions and strengthens the forces conducive to collapse.

The full political, military, and psychological implications of extended periods of slow growth are difficult to predict, but it is clear that lagging economic progress will create increasing difficulties for democratic governments. The past decade of economic problems has been associated with electoral shifts in many trilateral governments, with a growing emphasis on economic nationalism, and with a heightened sense of international tension. If the great depression formed part of the backdrop for the rise of fascist regimes and the second world war, it seems likely that continued recession would also encourage political demagogy and more authoritarian modes of political leadership. Authoritarian and totalitarian governments typically promise that they can better promote economic development. As our previous chapter pointed out, to blunt this appeal, our governments must show that economically as well as politically democracies do work.

ISSUES

As the above discussion implies, the overriding international economic issue is one of achieving stable and sustained economic growth. We believe such growth is also a key to the effectiveness of the trilateral countries in achieving social, political and security goals.

There is no comprehensive formula for sustained non-inflationary economic growth. Clearly confidence to invest and save by the private sector is an essential ingredient, and such confidence will not be achieved without private sector faith in the wisdom and consistency of public policies. This discussion, therefore, is oriented toward issues of public policy: how to achieve growth in the trilateral countries, taking due account of the links—and not least the debt issue—between developed and developing countries.

GROWTH IN THE TRILATERAL COUNTRIES

The economies of the trilateral countries are still recovering from the recent recession. Recovery has been most dramatic in the United States, where GNP, which fell by nearly 2 per cent in 1982, rose by about 3.5 per cent in 1983 and is expected to rise by about 5 per cent in 1984. Canada also has achieved a relatively rapid rate of economic recovery, but growth rates in Japan and Europe continue to lag behind.

There are a number of clouds on the economic horizon, which make it unclear whether or not the current economic recovery can be sustained into the medium-term future. The still overwhelming size of the U.S. economy makes its future the most critical, and it is here that we will first direct our attention.

The U.S. Budget Deficit
United States growth has been impressive, but it has been too dependent on expansionary fiscal policy, reflected in the huge U.S. budget deficit. To keep inflation in check, the Federal Reserve has had to maintain tight monetary policy, resulting in high real interest rates.

This macroeconomic mix skews economic activity away from investment and toward consumption.

Despite the recovery, the deficit, now running at an annual rate of
about $200 billion, or more than 5 per cent of the GNP, looks unlikely to
fall significantly in the foreseeable future. The U.S. Bipartisan Budget
Appeal (whose leading members include five former Secretaries of the
Treasury) expect that even on quite optimistic assumptions, budget
deficits are likely to remain in the range of 5-6 per cent of the GNP up to
1988 at least. This deficit, which was a fiscal stimulus to the U.S.
economy in 1983, may well be extremely dangerous if continued
throughout the 1980s.

For countries such as Japan, which have a very high propensity to
save, budget deficits of 5 or 6 per cent of the GNP should pose a lesser
problem: the private sector can lend 5 or 6 per cent of the GNP to the
public sector without cutting back on profitable investment in the
domestic private sector, or overseas. But the United States is not in this
position. The propensity to save is low: total private savings, net of
capital consumption, represent only 6-7 per cent of the GNP. The
upshot is that budget deficits of the present size absorb about three
quarters of all U.S. private savings.

One consequence of this situation is that productive investment is
discouraged: investment in new plant and machinery, and expenditures on research and development, are likely to be lower than they
would be if a larger proportion of the nation's savings were available to
finance them, and if interest rates were lower. The implications for the
growth of U.S. productivity in the medium to longer term are
ominous.

However, because of the size of the U.S. economy and the command-
ing role of the U.S. dollar in the international trade and financial
system, the effects of large U.S. budget deficits are much greater and
more pervasive than their effects on U.S. investment levels. Combined
with a monetary policy designed to keep the growth of the money
supply down to the figure thought to be consistent with a low inflation
rate, large budget deficits mean high interest rates. Real interest rates
(i.e. after adjusting for inflation) in the United States are in the 5-10 per
cent range; nominal rates are, of course, higher. One effect of these
high interest rates has been a huge inflow of capital into the United
States, which has resulted in a very big appreciation of the dollar, to a
level which by early 1984, according to many observers, was overvalued, on an effective exchange rate basis, by 20-30 per cent. The
consequences are predictable: a trade deficit which rose from $28
billion in 1981 to $36 billion in 1982 and $69 billion in 1983, and which is

expected to reach about $100 billion in 1984. Correspondingly, the current account deficit as a whole has already exceeded 1 per cent of GNP and is moving up towards 2 per cent—an incongruous situation for the world's largest developed country to be in. This rising current account deficit has, of course, helped to stimulate other countries' economies; but the decreasing American competitiveness which has been the main cause of it has also led to increasingly fierce protectionist pressures within America; and if America were to go protectionist on any signficant scale the outlook for the world economy would be dire.

High U.S. interest rates have forced other developed countries to keep their interest rates high too, for fear of an even greater decline in the value of their currencies in terms of the dollar, and the imported inflation which this would threaten. As a result, investment in these countries has been inhibited, just as it has in the United States itself. Even more serious has been the impact on the developing countries, and particularly those with large external debts. Under the system of variable interest rates on their external debt, the burden of servicing the debt has been higher than seemed likely when much of the debt was contracted; and since the debt is mainly denominated in dollars, the strength of the dollar has increased the local currency cost of debt service.

We believe that there clearly needs to be a shift in the fiscal/monetary mix in the United States, both to sustain a non-inflationary American recovery in the longer run and to avoid the negative by-products now troubling the world economy. It is doubtful whether the present mix can be maintained in the longer term anyway; either the deficit will have to be monetized through inflation or still higher and higher interest rates will be needed to attract more capital to cover increasingly onerous servicing of past debt. Tighter fiscal policy is essential to permit more flexibility on the monetary side, reduce interest rates, and free up capital for investment. There are some signs of movement: President Reagan announced early in 1984 a readiness to consider, on a bipartisan basis, measures to reduce the budget deficit by a total of $100 billion over the next three years. However, such a reduction—supposing that agreement on the necessary steps could be reached between the Administration and the Congress— would be much less than is required: it could still leave a budget deficit of around $150 billion in 1986-87. There is rarely an auspicious time for policy change or political compromise, particularly in the United States during election years, but the needs of the international community are urgent, and there are immense benefits for global stability in early action to reduce the budget deficit by much more than the United States is contemplating.

We do not intend here to recommend specific tax and spending proposals, but it is clear that sustained action on both fronts is needed to reduce the large U.S. structural deficits. On the spending side, benefits that go primarily to middle-income groups will either have to be reduced or financed by higher taxes or charges; but it is likely that at least some of these cuts in middle-class entitlement programs may take years before their effects are strongly felt. Like most trilateral governments, the United States is experiencing a rapid increase in the share of its elderly population, and this automatically translates into large and continuing expenditures, given present entitlements and cost-of-living increases in social security and medical care programs. Another area to be examined must be the defense budget, where in the view of some observers the rapid growth of spending during the last few years has in any case outstripped the ability of the defense community to efficiently use the new funding. Even more than adjustments to the entitlement programs, some changes in defense spending will take years, as forward commitments and contracts have already been budgeted through the late 1980s. Nevertheless, the longer-run implications of programs already started need careful review, and adjustments must begin to be made.

Japan and Western Europe

A more balanced U.S. fiscal/monetary macroeconomic mix will allow other trilateral governments to more freely adopt stimulative economic policies. At the same time, stronger growth elsewhere should prove very helpful to the United States. With growth, other trilateral countries will demand more imports which will help the U.S. trade balance; and their improved economic prospects should prove a source of attraction for domestic capital, which should strengthen their currencies *vis-à-vis* the dollar.

Of the other trilateral countries, Japan is probably in the best position to play a more positive role in stimulating its own and the world economy. There is considerable reluctance in Japan to boost the economy through an expansionary fiscal policy on the grounds that the budget deficit now equals about 25-30 per cent of the budget, that outstanding public debt represents more than 40 per cent of GNP, and that the servicing of this debt accounts for about 15 per cent of central government expenditures. Many foreign observers and some Japanese, however, point out that on the other hand Japan's propensity to save is unusually high and that surplus savings can finance government deficits as well as be channelled outward as foreign investment and aid. The fact that the 1984-85 budget is planned to rise by only half

of one per cent—the smallest increase since 1955—and that the projected cuts in direct taxes are to be offset by increases in indirect
taxation suggests that fiscal policy is still too cautious. Japan's economic
recovery continues to lag behind North America's, and given Japan's
massive merchandise trade surplus and continuing trade frictions with
its trilateral partners, an export-led recovery is internationally inexpe-
dient. An expansionary economic policy on the part of Japan is needed
in the mid-1980s.

In the monetary area, there has been some reduction of interest rates
to stimulate domestic investment, but this has been approached very
cautiously because it widens the gap betwen domestic and foreign
interest rates. The maintenance of a low rate of inflation (in 1984 about 2
per cent a year) is a high priority which should be continued; this is a
constraint on stimulative fiscal and monetary policies. Nevertheless,
the combination of a very low inflation rate and a large balance of
payments surplus on current account have put Japan in a strong
position to adopt a more expansionary macroeconomic stance.

More rapid growth in Japan can help to stimulate the world economy
through rising Japanese imports, particularly if Japan makes further
efforts to reduce the difficulties which other countries sometimes
encounter when attempting to export to Japan. Nevertheless, it seems
likely that Japan will continue to run balance of payments surpluses on
current account, and hence be an exporter of capital to the rest of the
world—a counterpart of the fact that its domestic savings are too large
to be accommodated at home even by a high rate of domestic investment and the current level of budget deficits. In these circumstances,
Japan could increase substantially its contributions to the international
financial institutions such as the IMF, the World Bank (including IDA)
and the regional development banks; and could also assist in rein-
vigorating Europe, by direct investment accompanied by an injection
of advanced technology and management skills. Finally, Japan should
continue its efforts toward internationalization of the yen, so that it
becomes a more important reserve and trading currency. Some encouraging measures in this direction were announced in late 1983, and
should be expeditiously implemented.

Europe must also play its part in promoting a global economic
recovery. Britain and West Germany in particular have been pursuing
unduly restrictive fiscal policies: on a full employment budget basis,
both countries were in 1984 running sizeable budget surpluses. This is
particularly true of Britain, where the unemployment rate is the highest for nearly fifty years. Sterling was, early in 1984, at its all-time low
against the dollar, and there is probably little scope for cuts in interest

rates until American interest rates come down; but there is scope for cuts in direct taxation to improve incentives and in indirect taxation to offset the inflationary effect of the higher import prices resulting from the strength of the dollar. There is also massive scope for increased investment in the country's decaying social and economic infrastructure.

The Deutschmark, too, by the start of 1984 had plumbed new depths against the dollar, but the scope for reducing interest rates in Germany is probably greater than in Britain. The German economy is fundamentally sound, the inflation rate—at less than 3 per cent—one of the lowest in the world, and the balance of payments improving. There is no reason why both fiscal and monetary policy should not be used to provide some increased impetus to Germany's so far sluggish recovery.

If Japan, Germany and Britain take concerted action to expand their economies, then other European countries which already have a grip on their inflation rates, whose current account is in balance or surplus, and whose capital markets are not overstrained by budget deficits, should not be afraid to join them. This applies, for instance, to Norway, Austria and Switzerland. Even France, whose attempt to expand on its own in 1981-82 led to a rapidly deteriorating current account and a run on the franc which forced it to abandon its expansionary policies after only a year, would be able to relax its austerity measures if coordinated expansion was undertaken by Japan and other European countries; and the incipient danger of France relapsing into increased industrial and agricultural protectionism would by the same token be reduced.

Nevertheless, the effectiveness of coordinated expansion by Western Europe and Japan is likely to be limited as long as real interest rates in the U.S. remain at their present level. If there is no sustained increase in investment in the trilateral countries because the cost of borrowing money is high in relation to the returns from investing it in physical assets, the present recovery will peter out, and the grim scenarios attendant upon slow growth in the OECD area will be in ever-increasing danger of turning into reality.

GROWTH IN THE DEVELOPING COUNTRIES

Too often the vital relationship between economic growth in the developed and in the developing worlds is overlooked by the politicians and the public in our countries. We have pointed out above the extent to which future growth in the developing countries depends on healthy economic advance in the trilateral world. The converse, of course, is also true. It has been estimated that a uniform 3 per cent reduction in growth in the developing countries would reduce OECD growth by 0.8 per cent. Developing countries provide the market for about one quarter of OECD exports. Part of the reason the recession following the second oil crisis was more severe than that following the first oil crisis is that demand in the developing countries, aggravated by the LDC debt crisis, was greatly reduced. Industrial production in the developed countries dropped by 4 percent between 1981 and 1982, reducing the demand for primary materials exported by many developing countries. At the same time, high interest rates increased the cost of holding inventories, while lower inflation lessened the attractiveness of commodities as hedges against inflation, further reducing demand. As a result, the prices of minerals, metals, fibers, timber, and rubber were sharply lower than in 1981. This in turn affected the developed world. Between 1981 and the first half of 1983, for example, the exports of the United States, Japan and the United Kingdom to Latin America were each reduced by more than 40 per cent; and West German exports to the same region declined by 33 per cent. The cost to trilateral states can be substantial. It has been estimated that the $8 billion fall in U.S. exports to Latin America from 1981 to 1982 cost between 100,000 and 130,000 manufacturing jobs in the United States.

The issues involved in growth in the developing world were carefully analyzed in the 1983 task force report to the Trilateral Commission on *Facilitating Development in a Changing Third World*. It is well, however, to review and update some of these conclusions as they are an integral part of any comprehensive strategy for restoring world economic growth.

Essential capital resources for Third World development come in three main forms: export earnings, foreign aid ("official development assistance", or ODA), and commercial (or non-concessional) capital flows. All three resources have been constrained by the recession.

As for export earnings, UNCTAD estimates the purchasing power of the exports of oil-importing developing countries (reflecting both volume and terms of trade) increased by 5.3 per cent annually from 1975 to 1980, but in 1981 the increase was only 0.9 per cent and in 1982, 0.5 per cent. In the case of the "least developed countries," the purchasing power of exports decreased by 5.5 per cent in 1981 and 3.7 per cent in 1982, following an average annual rate of increase of 4.8 per cent in the preceding half decade. This can be contrasted with the experience of the industrialized world, which also suffered from the worldwide recession, but less dramatically. While the export prices of developing countries' commodities dropped by 25 per cent over 1980-82, the prices of primary exports from industrialized countries declined by only 12.5

per cent. These figures mainly reflect lower demand for the primary products of developing countries. Moreover, manufactured exports are threatened by existing or potential trade barriers in the trilateral countries.

As developing countries industrialize, they become more valuable markets for the trilateral countries. Most studies show that increased North-South trade results in increasing employment in manufacturing for both areas. The trilateral countries should hold the line against further protectionism, and seek to expand access for the products of the developing countries, for example along the lines of the Generalized System of Preferences and the Lomé Convention agreements between the EEC and a group of African, Caribbean and Pacific countries.

Turning to ODA, the 1983 Trilateral Commission task force report referred to above noted a plateauing in the level of ODA despite increased needs, especially in the least developed countries. Many of the least developed countries are located in sub-Saharan Africa, which faces the appalling prospect of negative growth over the next decade unless there is a substantial increase in the flow of resources from outside. In this region mass starvation is an ever-present danger, life expectancy averages only 46 years, literacy is no more than 25 per cent, and governmental organization is extremely weak and must cope with a myriad of ethnic and social issues which would be serious enough challenges even with adequate economic growth. The trilateral governments should be devoting far more resources to this desperately deprived region of the world.

The previous task force report recommended both increasing the level of ODA and shifting its distribution more towards the neediest countries. We endorse these general recommendations. The results, however, have been disappointing. The centerpiece of international assistance efforts to low-income developing countries is the International Development Association (IDA), the soft-loan window of the World Bank, and IDA resources need to be increased. In recent negotiations, 31 of the 32 donors to IDA agreed on a three-year $12 billion replenishment, a figure which was the same as the previous IDA replenishment. The remaining donor, the United States, committed itself to only $2.25 billion. Given its 25 per cent share, this limited IDA-VII to only $9 billion, a substantial reduction. Clearly, there is a continuing need to convince the American Congress and Administration of its vital stake in expanded ODA. At the same time other trilateral countries which are prepared to increase their contributions to IDA should move ahead rapidly to do so. Japan, in particular, is in a good position to to this.

The LDC Debt Crisis

The LDC debt problem has received more active attention from the trilateral governments because it presented an immediate crisis to the international financial community. Another aspect, however, is the longer-term question of adequate capital for middle income countries for which non-concessional loans had become a mainstay of financing current account deficits created by rapid economic growth.

The origins of the debt crisis lay in the rapid expansion of commercial lending to certain developing countries following the first oil crisis. This lending was widely regarded at the time as an appropriate means of re-cycling the OPEC current account surplus and of covering the oil bills of developing countries while they adjusted to higher import costs. Morgan Guaranty has noted that for the 21 major borrowers (those which had accumulated debts of at least $3 billion by mid-1982), outstanding bank loans had increased at an average annual rate of more than 30 per cent from the mid-1970s to the second oil shock of 1979. Easily the main recipients of these loans were Latin American countries, especially Mexico and Brazil. Latin America absorbed two-thirds of all Euromarket bank lending to developing countries and the commercial banks accounted for more than two-thirds of the capital inflow into Latin America over the past decade.

Because the overall growth rates of borrowers remained strong, because export growth proceeded rapidly and because, owing to high inflation, real interest rates remained low, the debt servicing required remained well within their capacities in the mid-1970s. This situation changed after the second oil crisis. Exports stagnated because of the worldwide recession, and since most debts had been contracted at variable rates of interest, the escalation of real interest rates sent debt servicing demands shooting upward. Real interest rates increased from 1.65 per cent in 1978 to more than 7 per cent during the first two quarters of 1982. Still, misjudging the severity and length of the recession, borrowing continued at almost the same pace into 1982, although an increased share represented short-term loans, which need to be rolled over more often and hence render the borrower more vulnerable to a change in the willingness of lenders to continue lending.

Confidence in continued lending to developing countries, especially the large Latin American borrowers, collapsed in 1982 when, in August, Mexico became the first large debtor to suspend debt-service payments. Several other countries, notably Brazil, were soon forced to seek debt rescheduling. A much more serious crisis was averted by action by the central banks of the trilateral countries (working through the Bank for International Settlements) and the IMF, which also put strong pressure on commercial banks to continue sufficient lending. However, as a precondition for IMF assistance, debtor nations have nearly always been required to pursue deflationary policies at home and cut imports. In many cases, these policies have been successful in producing trade surpluses, but they have come at considerable economic sacrifice (declining GNP in two or three successive years), which is unlikely to be sustained for long without creating serious social upheaval or political unrest. There is, moreover, the danger of a downward spiral: as one country reduces its imports, other countries' exports fall, and they in turn may be forced to deflate and cut their imports, with further effects on other countries. Brazil is a case in point. Its exports to industrialized countries fell by 3 per cent in 1982, but its exports to oil-importing developing countries dropped by about 19 per cent.

High levels of indebtedness for some Latin American countries will continue throughout the coming decade, rendering these countries continually vulnerable to changes in export earnings, interest rates, and perceptions of their credit-worthiness. At the present time, rescue operations by the banks, international agencies, and governments do little more than stave off an ultimate economic or political reckoning, buying time for the debtors to continue to cover their interest payments, if somewhat tardily. The creditors have little incentive to provide much in the way of capital beyond what is needed to meet past over-commitments. It is unrealistic, however, to expect the countries which have been relying on large infusions of commercial capital to suddenly become longer-term net exporters of capital as they struggle to pay back past debt obligations. In fact, in 1982 there was a net flow from developing countries to developed countries' banks of $7 billion; this rose to $21 billion in 1983. Thus a critical question in the medium term, one with implications for both middle income and trilateral economies, is how to assure adequate capital infusions for growth, assuming that commercial bank lending will be much more restricted than in the past.

As was pointed out earlier, one of the most critical variables determining the ability of the developing countries to service their debt will be the growth rate of the developed countries. If the OECD countries grow at around 3.5 per cent a year between now and 1990, the Morgan Guaranty projections show a rise in the external debt of the 21 main debtor countries from an estimated $580 billion at the end of 1984 to $820 billion in 1990—a serious situation, but one that ought to be containable. If OECD growth is only 2.5 per cent a year, on the other hand, the debt is projected to rise by 80 per cent to $1,050 billion—an outcome that is barely conceivable. But if OECD growth were to be around 4.5 per cent, the external debt in 1990 would actually be lower than it is at present. In short, the importance of a reasonably rapid and sustained rate of growth in the trilateral countries to the continued stability of the international trading and financial system can scarcely be exaggerated.

Other variables, such as the terms of trade of the developing countries and the trend of oil prices, are also of great importance, but are not under the control of the trilateral countries. But what happens to interest rates is also of critical importance, and these are to a very large extent under the control of the trilateral countries, and particularly the United States. A 2 per cent fall in the London inter-bank lending rate (LIBOR) would reduce the external debt of the main 21 countries in 1990 by around $100 billion; correspondingly, a 2 per cent rise would raise it by around $100 billion. Thus these projections strengthen the argument, advanced earlier, for a reduction in the size of the American budget deficit and hence a fall in U.S. and world interest rates.

Thus our view is that the problem of international debt is containable provided that sensible macroeconomic policies are pursued by the trilateral countries, and particularly by the United States. But it would be injudicious to leave the matter there: some sort of back-up solution may be needed. Many proposals have been put forward, including schemes for insuring the loans made by the private banks, or for some international body to take over their developing country loans at a discount. Proposals of various kinds have also been made for increasing the callable capital of the international banking institutions, particularly the Inter-American Development Bank, and for increasing the gearing ratio for World Bank loans. These schemes, or any other schemes, would involve costs of some sort or another being borne by someone. Our view is that if proposals of this kind need to be put into operation—and we are in favor of them being further studied—it should be recognized that all those parties involved bear some of the blame for the severity of the international debt problem. Many developing countries borrowed too much, too soon, and sometimes failed to use the money in the way most calculated to benefit their economies. Many of the private banks jettisoned normal rules of banking prudence in seeking big profits in the developing countries. And many of the governments of the trilateral countries did too little to discourage—and sometimes too much to encourage—this reckless increase of their banks' loan exposure in particular developing countries. In consequence, all three parties will have to bear some of the costs of putting the situation to rights: the developing countries, some degree of austerity; the banks, some writing-off of loans; the taxpayers of the OECD countries, increased funding of the international financial institutions. Unless the debt problem is solved by a combination of rapid growth and lower interest rates, these costs must be borne: any attempt to evade them could precipitate a genuine international financial crisis.

INTERNATIONAL MONETARY SYSTEM

The flexible exchange rate system has had negative effects on the world economy, including rate volatility and over-shooting. This has increased adjustment problems of national economies. Nor have national economies been insulated from the national economic policies of other countries by flexible exchange rates as in theory should have happened. Given, however, the huge amounts of footloose capital free to move from one currency to another, it is impossible to return to fixed rates, nor could fixed rates have coped with the crises of the past decade.

It has been suggested that a large fund of dollars, marks, and yen be put together for intervening to stabilize the exchange rates of major currencies. Intervention can smooth out fluctuations, but it cannot adjust the basic problem of misalignment of major currencies. In the longer term, greater stability of exchange rates depends on greater stability in the domestic economies of the trilateral countries and in a consistent set of policies. This implies the need for the coordination of macroeconomic policies.

It is clear that by early 1984 exchange rates were seriously out of line. The dollar was probably overvalued, compared with its fundamental equilibrium exchange rate, by 20-30 per cent. The effective exchange rate of sterling— though not its rate against the dollar—was also too high. The yen and the Deutschmark, by contrast, were clearly undervalued. These misalignments are mainly the consequence of inappropriate macroeconomic policies, particularly in the United States and to a lesser extent in Britain. An important part of the kind of coordination of economic policies which we believe—as we argue in Chapter V—must be launched through the summit process will be agreement on policies which will bring exchange rates into line with each other. Once that has been done, continuous monitoring of exchange rate movements will be needed, and action must be taken to prevent particular currencies from moving outside the zones which are agreed to be appropriate.

International Trading System

No discussion of the world economy would be complete without consideration of the international trading system, now under a good deal of stress. Protectionism was one of the roots of the world depression of the 1930s and liberalized trade was one of the mainsprings of the sustained economic growth through much of the postwar period, yet there are an increasing number in our countries who advocate direct or indirect forms of protection in the mistaken belief that it can promote economic growth or safeguard jobs.

The GATT has been remarkably successful in reducing many tariff barriers and beginning to regulate non-tariff barriers, but the complexities of the international trading system have grown. Some of these new complexities include the expansion of intra-firm trade, competitive export credit schemes, and the growth of trade in services. Matters once considered almost entirely under the discretion of national governments—taxation systems, industrial incentives, the nature of government-business relations, inspection and licensing procedures, and health and safety regulations to mention only a few—are now regarded as closely related to industrial competitiveness and to the basic fairness of the system.

Governments are resorting to a variety of unilateral or bilateral "extra-legal" measures, unregulated by more general principles such as the non-discriminatory trade principles underlying the GATT.

Strengthening the GATT system is an essential element in the coming decade's international economic agenda. We do not underestimate the difficulties involved, but the most recent Tokyo Round of GATT multilateral trade negotiations, undertaken in an unpromising atmosphere, yielded some surprising achievements in a number of new areas. The trilateral countries should recommit themselves to the principles of GATT in deeds as well as words. In particular, they should take action along the following lines: 1) they should initiate negotiations on trade in services and on safeguards; 2) they should examine the possibility of converting, within 4 to 5 years, their extra-legal restrictions taken outside the GATT into tariffs covered by GATT, or dispense with them entirely; 3) they should seek to establish a new GATT committee on industrial policies, a grey area ill-covered by GATT, so that trade-distorting effects of these policies are recognized, monitored, and minimized; 4) they should seek to strengthen the GATT dispute-settlement mechanisms.

CONCLUSION

In this chapter we have described as essential a number of measures to increase growth, to deal with the developing country debt problem, and to revitalize the international monetary and trading systems. These include a substantial reduction in the U.S. budget deficit, a fiscal stimulus in other trilateral countries—particularly in Japan, Britain and Germany, and a major increase in Japanese development aid. However, economic policies in themselves are a necessary but not a sufficient condition of sustained economic prosperity. A political and security environment conducive to saving and investment is also required.

The two most disastrous economic shocks of the 1970s had their direct origins in political crises. The first massive oil price increase was triggered by the 1973 Arab-Israeli war, and the second by the Iranian revolution of 1979. Earlier, the Vietnam War had generated growing inflation in the United States, and weakened the capacity of the United States to act as the anchor of the Bretton Woods fixed exchange rate system. Conversely, the rapid recovery and growth in Western Europe and Japan in the 1950s and 1960s owed much to the political decisions of the United States to help these countries economically, while assuming primary responsibility for collective security.

Clearly the international economic agenda and the political/security agenda of the trilateral nations are closely intertwined. It is to the latter that we now turn.

IV. COOPERATION OR FRAGMENTATION: THE POLITICAL RESPONSE

The central issue in this decade's foreign policy agenda for the trilateral countries can be stated quite simply: it is the need to create mechanisms and processes by which we can avert the threat of nuclear war, social breakdowns, regional conflicts and economic deterioration while capitalizing on the opportunities for improved international order. The consummate challenge is to shape a more effective world system, responding sympathetically to the reality of the new global political awakening.

In the first part of this chapter we shall examine some of the most important elements and trends in the contemporary global picture. Some are encouraging: the expanding scaffolding of multilateral institutions, the sharing of scientific and technical data for the betterment of humanity, the waning of the global appeal of the Soviet model, and the compelling nature of freedom and human rights. Other aspects of the global picture represent major, or even catastrophic dangers: the risk of nuclear war, social breakdown in the Third World, debilitating regional crises, and strains in trilateral cooperation.

ELEMENTS AND TRENDS IN THE CONTEMPORARY GLOBAL PICTURE

The Institutional Scaffolding

At the end of the second world war the United States emerged as the most powerful nation on earth and as the leading force for the development of global and collective peace-keeping machinery. Frustrated by the defects in the League of Nations charter, and distressed by America's earlier isolationism, the war-weary founders of the United Nations banked on the Security Council's entitlement under Articles 42 and 43 in Chapter 7 to ensure collective international action to preserve the peace. When the Security Council ran afoul of the realities of the Cold War and two superpower vetos, the role of the General Assembly was expanded into international security affairs. Epitomized by the Uniting for Peace Resolution in 1950, it formalized the right of the General Assembly to intervene when the Security Council was deadlocked. But this power to take multinational action other than through the Security

Council was never used again; effectively the United Nations has had to live within the constraints of the veto power.

Subsequent U.N. efforts to prevent or contain war have been more successful than is usually acknowledged within the trilateral countries. The U.N. was active in Greece from 1947 to 1954, between Israel and the Arabs in 1948, in Indonesia from 1947 to 1950, and in Kashmir in 1949. After these early observer roles, the U.N. peace-keeping contingents gradually interposed themselves as armed contingents between belligerent forces: between Egypt and Israel in Gaza and the Sinai, in the Congo from 1960 to 1964, between Greece and Turkey in Cyprus in 1964, and in the Sinai and the Golan Heights from 1973. In Lebanon, although the United Nations International Force has been reasonably successful in the South since 1978, the difficulty of multinational peace-keeping divorced from the U.N. has been all too tragically evident in Beirut. The trilateral countries must consider urgently how to contribute in ways which will make U.N. peacekeeping more effective.

Peace-keeping is not the only U.N. activity contributing to the emerging global system. Some United Nations agencies have a more impressive record, among them the World Health Organization, the International Labor Organization, and UNICEF. Virtually each one is a first attempt in world history to organize international programs to benefit all humanity. Additional activities—the U.N.'s three Development Decades, its three Conferences on the Law of the Sea, and the 1974 and 1975 Special Sessions, which were largely devoted to a New International Economic Order—enhanced mutual cooperation on emerging world problems but because of a lack of resources or political consensus generally fell short of making a major impact. The notable exception was the series of discussions between 1958 and 1980 on the Law of the Sea, which formulated five strong conventions which are the basis of current sea law.

More regional organizations, born of the "institutional revolution" after the second world war, also contribute to peace-keeping as well as study and problem-solving. Those with a broad if imperfect competence include the Organization of American States, the Organization of African Unity, the Organization for Economic Cooperation and Development grouping 24 industrial states, and various new committees involving the 47 countries of the Commonwealth. The European Community is more politically oriented than it was, while the more recent Association of South East Asian Nations has a nascent potential for broader strategic cooperation. Both the EEC and ASEAN started with an emphasis on economic cooperation that has grown into political cooperation. As against this, the Andean group of countries has been weakened by the withdrawal of Chile, and the East African Community collapsed—though more recently relations have shown signs of improvement.

Fourteen specialized organizations coordinate many of the world's social, technical, economic and human requirements: the International Monetary Fund, the World Bank group, the Universal Postal Union, and the International Civil Aviation Organization, among others. In addition, 58 developing countries and the EEC formalized in Lomé I and II an international reciprocal trade agreement, while the General Agreement on Tariffs and Trade remains a unique international instrument which embodies rules covering most of world trade.

In this manner, an expanding scaffolding of multilateral institutions reinforces the emerging global understanding of the need for such wider cooperation. However, it must also be noted that the effectiveness of existing institutions tends to be limited to functional issues, and the more traditional political and ideological conflicts among nations have not been susceptible to effective international mediation. There is little doubt that if the trilateral countries could achieve consensus amongst themselves and take such agreement into all their different international bodies the power and influence of those bodies would be strengthened immeasurably.

The Sharing of Scientific and Technical Data to Better Humanity

The institutional framework of international cooperation is greatly enhanced by the growing scientific capacity of mankind to improve its condition. Scientific and technological breakthroughs cover almost all areas of inquiry, and involve interconnected computer processes, hybrid grains, and medical advances. Vast quantities of data—that precious "seed" which promises so much future understanding—are instantaneously transmitted internationally by telephone, telex, electronic transfers, satellite, and computer—when once only letters and telegraph signalled the world's needs. Skills are transmitted too via project consultants who provide technical expertise, training and advice to remote regions.

Medical advances have reduced those scourges of humanity—malaria, smallpox, and cholera—by the introduction of worldwide disease monitoring and research. Such an emphasis has been placed worldwide on building a basic health infrastructure, improving education, family planning and proper nutrition that mortality rates in the Third World have fallen to 10-20 per 1,000, rates which the developed world did not attain before 1900, or in some cases before 1925.

Improved technology for food production helped to double the world output of cereals between 1950 and 1980. The Green Revolution—built upon foundation-funded research on high-yield varieties—boosted production tremendously, first in Mexican corn and wheat in the 1940s and then in Southeast Asian rice in the 1960s. Although no panacea—and sometimes having adverse effects on the distribution of income—these miracle crops provided hope when desperately needed and offered concrete proof that the returns from even a relatively small financial expenditure in agricultural research can be very high: in Mexico, for example, the annual rate of return on wheat research was 750 percent.

The Waning of the Global Appeal of the Soviet Model

For a number of decades after the 1917 Revolution the Soviet experiment was seen by many as the wave of the future. It was, therefore, only natural that in the wake of the decolonization following the second world war many of the new states in Asia and Africa turned toward the Soviet Union for guidance on their socio-economic development. The Soviet Union was perceived by many in the developing world, and also by many theorists in the developed world, as offering a highly relevant and effective model of rapid modernization and industrialization. This greatly enhanced Soviet political influence and gave the Soviet Union added international standing.

In recent years, that appeal has greatly declined. The Soviet system is today viewed as bureaucratically sterile and a stifler of freedom, innovation and diversity. A number of the developing countries have also come to challenge conventional development patterns and to realize that it is at least as important to develop their agricultural potential as to focus on heavy industrial growth. They have been very disappointed by the level of development assistance, in contrast to military aid, proffered by the Soviet Union. Indeed, Soviet development aid has continued to shrink in the course of the last decade, and today the Soviets contribute a surprisingly small amount to Third World development, considering the Soviet GNP. Financial assistance by the Soviet Union and COMECON members to LDCs amounted, over the last few years, to less than $2 billion per year, compared with $28 billion (0.38 per cent of their combined GNP) given by the OECD countries in 1982. In that year the United States gave $8.2 billion (0.27 per cent of GNP), Japan $3.0 billion (0.29 per cent), Britain $1.8 billion (0.37 per cent), France—excluding overseas territories and dependencies—$2.6 billion (0.49 per cent), Germany $3.2 billion (0.48 per cent), Italy $0.8 billion (0.24 per cent) and Canada $1.2 billion (0.42 per cent of GNP).

The decline in the appeal of the Soviet experience as a model of development has been paralleled by a wider appreciation of its extraordinary social costs. Moreover, despite forced savings and large-scale regimentation, and notwithstanding Soviet achievements in space, in sophisticated military technology and some aspects of industrial production, the USSR has not been as successful as many assumed in the immediate post-war era. According to a comparative study of development by Professor Cyril Black of Princeton University: "In the perspective of fifty years, the comparative ranking of the USSR in composite economic and social indices per capita has probably not changed significantly. So far as the rather limited available evidence permits a judgement, the USSR has not overtaken or surpassed any country on a per capita basis since 1917 with the possible exception of Italy, and the nineteen or twenty countries that rank higher than Russia today in this regard also ranked higher in 1900 and 1919."

The resulting scepticism regarding communist doctrinal solutions has not prompted the Third World mechanically to adopt the free market doctrines of either Japan or Western Europe, or North America for that matter, but rather to search for its own indigenous solutions. This contributes to global economic pluralism and produces economic circumstances more comparable to the practice of the trilateral countries.

The Compelling Nature of Freedom and Human Rights

Political freedom is a key issue in areas as different as Poland, the Philippines, Chile, the Middle East, and Southern Africa, and attempts to achieve it take a variety of forms. In the political realm, a number of countries have made a remarkable transition from authoritarianism to democracy. Portugal and Spain provide the most impressive examples; their shift is a vindication of the democratic appeal. Even under less than ideal conditions, Argentina has recently made an impressive start in its return to democracy.

The "basic human needs" approach adopted by many multilateral and bilateral aid donors since the early 1970s is also a reflection of enhanced concern with human rights. These are development efforts geared primarily towards the individual—emphasizing food production and nutrition, rural development, population planning and health, and education. Similarly, since the U.N.'s Universal Declaration in 1948 and subsequent conventions, intergovernmental efforts have been devoted to securing agreements enhancing the protection of human rights. The Helsinki Agreement, or the Final Act of the Conference on Security and Cooperation in Europe, was signed at the highest levels of government in 1975 by the United States, Canada and 33 European countries after three years of discussion. "Basket III" of this agreement deals with cooperation in humanitarian and other fields. It emphasizes the free movement of people through family reunification, information and ideas. It has placed communist governments under collective international pressure to mitigate their arbitrary controls at the follow-up conferences of Belgrade and Madrid.

Other more ad hoc efforts emphasising individual rights include Western concern over Soviet treatment of its ethnic and religious minorities, particularly the Jews. This is perhaps most publicly emphasized through the Jackson-Vanik Amendment to the U.S.'s 1974 Trade Act. This prohibits the extension of U.S. government credits and Most Favored Nation trade status to any communist country which restricts or is not moving towards free emigration of its citizens.

Third World military struggles also threaten to negate some of the political gains on the human rights front. Between 1960 and 1982, 65 major wars (with recorded deaths of 1,000 or more) occurred in which almost 11 million people died. Three-quarters of these deaths were associated with civil wars—Vietnam from 1961 to 1973 (2 million), Cambodia from 1975 to 1978 (2 million), Nigeria from 1967 to 1970 (2 million) and Bangladesh in 1971 (1.5 million). Civilian and military deaths were approximately equal in the 1960s, but more recently civilian deaths have outnumbered military ones by a ratio of three to one. Aside from the massive individual abrogations of human rights associated with wars and insurrections, dozens of coups have occurred since 1960—34 in 13 Central and South American countries alone. The military is also often the major perpetrator of human rights violations, and its sway is increasing. According to Freedom House of New York City, by 1982, 52 of 113 developing countries were under military domination, most frequently without basic civic and legal rights. In all, in 1984, Freedom House characterized 58 states (41 per cent of the world's population) as "not free", 56 states (23 per cent of the world's population) as "partly free", and only 52 states (36 per cent of the world's population) as living in "free" societies.

A major negative change in the early 1980s was the decreased emphasis on human rights in the foreign policies of trilateral countries, particularly the United States and Britain. Unlike the Carter Presidency, whose emphasis on human rights encouraged a worldwide renaissance of interest, the Reagan Administration's lack of rhetorical enthusiasm and its strong support of countries with admittedly poor human rights records have diverted attention from this critical issue. The worldwide recession has also overshadowed human rights concerns, and made apparent trade-offs between order and freedom more difficult to justify and achieve.

These elements contain the potential for significant progress in improving the world condition. However, before we can become too sanguine, we must recognize the gravity of the serious dangers that increasingly threaten the world.

Nuclear and Conventional Warfare

In less than 45 minutes, some 220 million human beings could be killed through a first strike/second strike response limited to the territory of the two superpowers. An additional 150-180 million West Europeans and Japanese might also die, if the Soviets were to use their SS-20s to attack major military targets close to heavily populated areas in West Europe and Japan. The horrendous possibility of superpower nuclear conflict represents a threat so awesome that its full implications are almost impossible to anticipate and assimilate. The threat is, nevertheless, very real.

Increasingly complex nuclear weapons systems are being developed and deployed. Three other states—China, France and Britain—are also overtly enchancing their nuclear capabilities. It is only a matter of time before competition for military supremacy in space becomes intense, with control over space central to military preponderance on earth. The management of a stable military relationship in this context is bound to become more difficult. The possibility of war through an escalation of a small-scale military confrontation or some human or technical inadvertence is certainly increasing, given the number, complexity and deployment of a large variety of strategic, intermediate and battlefield nuclear weapons. Last but not least is the mechanism for controlling a crisis. Little is known of Soviet rules of engagement, and such recent incidents as the shooting down of the KAL 007 flight have given rise to uneasiness regarding Soviet command procedures.

Proliferation also is a growing problem. To date, the Non-Proliferation Treaty has not been signed by these nuclear-capable states: Argentina, Brazil, India, Israel, Pakistan, South Africa and Spain. Several are in a precariously exposed political position and might be tempted *in extremis* to use nuclear weapons. Although after almost 40 years the nuclear weapons "club" only numbers five states, at least 40 countries now have the technical ability to make their own weapons, and it is imperative that they all be formally part of the non-proliferation process.

Terrorist organizations are also to be feared, for it is only a matter of time before some of these engage in truly technologically sophisticated acts of terror. Crudely produced nuclear weapons could be devastating in small countries or large urban centers.

Chemical and biological warfare cannot be ruled out either. Despite continued talks between the United States and the USSR, chemical weapons appear to have been used in Laos, Cambodia, Afghanistan, and the Gulf War. Inexpensive and easy to make and store, they may increasingly become tempting alternatives for gaining territory and decimating populations, especially in the Third World, or as a tool of organized terrorism.

An Insidious Danger: Social Breakdown in the Third World

A less dramatic but more pervasive threat is that of major social-political breakdowns in Third World societies increasingly unable to cope with problems beyond their capabilities.

The most insidious danger is demographic, for it threatens to undo every other gain in health, medicine and technology. Although the birth rate has actually declined in all regions of the Third World since 1960, and this reduction appears to have accelerated, the world's population will exceed 6 billion by the year 2000, and probably 10 to 15 billion before a stationary level can be achieved. This means 2.2 billion people in China and India together by the end of the century, and a five-fold increase in Africa by 2075. The problem will be compounded in the developing countries by the continued explosive growth of urbanization. In 1950, 130 million people in developing countries lived in cities of 100,000 or more. By 1975 the figure had risen to 480 million; by 2000 it is expected to be over 1 billion. Fifteen or twenty cities in developing countries will contain more than 10 million people by the end of the century; some will contain more than 20 million, or even 30 million. This continued rapid urban growth will put enormous pressures on the organization of government and the provision of adequate food, shelter, jobs, water supplies, sanitation and health care. It is unlikely that their societies will be capable of employing or supporting this vast increase in population, unless a larger proportion of the population can be productively employed in agriculture.

Another alarming feature of the situation is the very high dependency ratio in the Third World. There, this ratio—the number of people below 15 and above 65 divided by the number of people between those ages—is approximately 70 per cent, versus 50 per cent in the developed world. This means that the income earned by the active population in the Third World must be divided many more ways than in the developed world.

The problem is fundamentally one of food and energy. Several events have combined to make food prospects especially bleak: the Soviet Union's decision in 1972 in effect to abandon "self-sufficiency" and become the world's largest cereal buyer; a rise in cereal imports by many developing countries; a decrease in the world's cereal reserves from the high point of 103 days consumption in 1968 to a level of perhaps 30 or so in 1984, below the minimum required for world food security as assessed by key international bodies; a significant rise in average nominal world cereal prices which slightly declined from 1950 to 1972, but which tripled from 1972 to 1974, and which have risen again in average terms—although wheat and rice prices are below their 1980 high; an annual rate of food production which increases scarcely faster than the population; and a dangerous overdependence of Third World citizens upon North American grains, given the fact that 60 per cent of their daily caloric intake is based on cereals. Given climatic instability, this dependence by roughly 500 million people is a serious and too-often overlooked risk. Already, at least 300 million are chronically malnourished, with one billion of the world's citizens, on an average day, not receiving an adequate calorie intake.

The world's "other energy crisis", wood shortage rather than oil shortage, is exacerbated by population growth and is already radically altering the world's ecosystem, causing untold suffering for millions. "Non-commercial" energies are still used by half the world in preparing food, and in Africa they equal two-thirds of total energy production, while in some countries (Nepal, Tanzania, Mali) they account for 90 per cent or more. Since wood provides 85 per cent of "non-commercial" energy used, its use is the source of a worldwide deforestation such that, according to the Global 2000 Report, by the year 2020 "virtually all the physically accessible forests in the less developed countries are expected to have been cut." If present trends continue, a full 40 per cent of the animal and plant varieties alive today will be extinct by the end of the century as their habitats disappear.

Debilitating Regional Crises

In such a climate, ethnic rivalries, famines, border wars and the messianic fervor of Muslim fundamentalism may prove overpowering to societies strained beyond the capacity of their systems. Several regional crises are already critical; under the conditions described above, it will become all the more imperative to defuse them. If poorly handled, they will adversely affect Western interests and are likely to produce dangerous East-West conflict. The Middle East and Persian

Gulf, Central America, Southern Africa and Eastern Europe are crisis areas in which the stakes for both East and West are high. They are all born of complex political, social, military and economic difficulties, none is easily "solveable" and some carry the risk of nuclear escalation.

Recent examples of increasingly dangerous regional conflicts, which the international community was able neither to prevent nor to terminate quickly, include Israel's military operations in Lebanon, as well as the continued Syrian intrusion; prolonged violence in Cambodia; the conflict over the Falkland Islands; and the increasingly destructive war of attrition which has now lasted for more than three years between Iran and Iraq.

The dangerous potential of these conflicts has been increased by the Soviet Union's emergence as a superpower, with its growing capabilities for influence and power projection. According to a recent count, during the first 20 years after the second world war, some degree of Soviet military presence occurred in fewer than 20 incidents around the world. Since 1973, however, some 67 incidents of Soviet military projection into Third World conflicts have taken place. This increased inclination to become directly involved greatly enhances the possibility of an American-Soviet clash occurring in the context of some Third World conflict or social collapse.

Strains in Trilateral Cooperation
The world's best hope is a concerted international effort to address the myriad of issues which threaten the globe. The trilateral countries encompass 70 percent of the world's GNP, include nine of the 10 wealthiest countries, and uniquely possess the technological resources and trained manpower capable of successfully addressing these issues. They have the tools to pull the world back as it approaches the edge of the precipice. However, political, procedural, and practical difficulties so undermine that capacity that radical change in our procedures and conduct must occur.

Unfortunately, there is reason to worry about the ability of the trilateral countries to rise to the challenge. We continue to be faced by an incapacity to move from crisis-management to long-term problem-solving. In addition, trilateral tensions over trade issues and the temptation of protectionism encourage unilateral national attempts to handle problems which can only be dealt with on a global basis. Conflicts on policy issues between and within trilateral states strain relations, while the American political system grows progressively more labored as it attempts to reconcile domestic political exigencies with foreign affairs. None of this bodes well for a successful and concerted effort to meet the needs described above.

Particularly poisonous for trilateral relations is the prospect of growing disparity in the socio-economic performance of the three trilateral regions. Unless the countries of the European Community take steps to enhance their scientific and technological development, it appears likely that Europe will be unable to keep pace with America's and Japan's plunge into the technetronic age. This will not only intensify Western Europe's socio-economic problems and heighten protectionist pressures but make the closed and backward Soviet-East European markets increasingly the outlet for Western Europe's less innovative industries. Moreover, economic difficulties within Europe, especially if public opinion blames them on the United States, will further intensify concerns aroused by the debate about nuclear weapons. Some will be increasingly tempted to blend economic resentment with political neutralism. It will require considerable skill from Western European political leaders if further strains in U.S.-West European security links are not to develop and increasing trading tensions emerge between Europe and Japan. It will also require from U.S. and Japanese politicians the vision to understand that a technologically inferior Western Europe will add to the political instability of the world in ways which will soon also rebound against the American and Japanese people.

ISSUES

The role of the trilateral countries will be decisive in shaping a more effective international system. Realism—not arrogance—dictates that this fact be acknowledged, and that it serve as the point of departure for responsible action. In most fields critical to the world's survival, the democratic and technologically advanced trilateral countries are the major locomotives of global progress: political, scientific, economic and intellectual. The original hopes for the Third World have been dissipated by its disunity and uneven economic performance, its wars and its leadership struggles. However, this calls for even greater concern over the future of the Third World and for more intense efforts to help cooperatively in its development. Unfortunately, at this stage the communist world is retrenching its aid to the Third World and confining it primarily to regimes with which it is politically associated.

In this context, the trilateral countries must widen the scope of cooperation among like-minded states, even at the cost of alienating some of their domestic constituencies. However, creating a Western domestic consensus for international reform, especially the formation and encouragement of like-minded groups across national boundaries and across domestic schisms, is critical—for in this process there will be no quick fixes. Only a protracted search can offer us the means by which we can begin to affect worldwide trends which have taken deep root over decades. In this process, continuity across administrations which is firmly rooted in a domestic consensus for international reform is of critical importance.

It is important in this process of widening cooperation also to engage China. Since the early 1940s the Chinese have desired to be a beacon for the Third World. Although rejected in their bid for leadership of the Non-Aligned Movement, China is held in high esteem by many states which must undertake radical social restructuring within the limits of very scare resources. A China more constructively engaged in multilateral cooperation would boost the chances of the trilateral countries' efforts to shape a more stable international order. It is essential to stress in this connection that China is an important independent force in world affairs, and relations between China and the trilateral countries should not be conditioned mainly by the exigencies of the East-West conflict.

Relations with the Soviet Union

To give the global leadership that is required the trilateral countries must first learn to live constructively with the inevitable differences among them regarding their relations with the Soviet Union. Japan, Western Europe, Canada and the United States perceive the Soviet Union differently due to their different geographical positions, their different historical experiences and their different economic and trading relationships. It is almost inevitable that their leaders and public opinions will place different values and priorities on the defense, economic and even social aspects of their respective relationships with the Soviet Union. Except in conditions of an overt Soviet military challenge, it is quite likely that these divergences will continue and perhaps even widen. Each of the three regions recognizes the military nature of the Soviet threat, but they often disagree on the nature of the political and economic threats, and how to assess and deal with them. For example, the trilateral states had divergent viewpoints over Soviet intervention in Afghanistan and the extent of Soviet involvement with the military in Poland, and those differences were not helped by the continued U.S. pressure on Europe over the Soviet pipeline, while the United States itself signed a new long-term cereals sale agreement with the USSR.

The trilateral countries must learn to live with these different perceptions, in effect agreeing to disagree, while shaping mechanisms to try and reduce the areas of disagreement. The Europeans, Japanese and Canadians should not conclude that American concentration on the antagonistic aspects of the U.S.-Soviet relationship reflects a dangerous crusading spirit. Americans must come to appreciate that European history and geography mean that their complex relationships with Russia should not be automatically labeled as neutralism or characterized as "Finlandization". Because the trilateral states have too often not acknowledged these differences in perception, divisive policy disagreements have developed.

Yet the reality is of growing interdependence between Western Europe, North America and Japan in the area of security. The deployment of the Soviet SS-20s against both Western Europe and the Far East reinforces the proposition that political and economic coordination among the trilateral countries will increasingly have to include the area of security.

If trilateral fragmentation is not to occur, there must be limits to the divergence in their relationships. This is particularly true of fundamental commitments to common needs—such as NATO. There has been a firm demonstration of this commitment in Italy, Britain and West Germany implementing NATO's decision to start deploying Cruise and Pershing II missiles in the face of major public protests. Since it was Europe that took the initiative in asking for a U.S. response to the SS-20 deployment it would have been peculiarly corrosive of the Atlantic Alliance if the Western Europeans had backed off deployment and been seen to have succumbed to a Soviet veto of any U.S. deployment. It is important in this context to make certain that any resolution of the SS-20 issue insofar as the interests of Western Europe are concerned does not disregard the equally important security interests of Japan. It has been a striking affirmation of the interdependence of the trilateral countries in strategic matters that in the INF negotiations with the Soviet Union the United States resisted at all stages, with full Western European support, an agreement which would have allowed the redeployment of SS-20 missiles targeted against Western Europe to Asia.

A new and important aspect of this Atlantic-Pacific security interdependence involves the independent role of China. China at present ties down 25 per cent of the Soviet defense effort, including 46 Soviet divisions, on the Sino-Soviet frontier, whereas in 1960 there were only 12 divisions on that frontier.

Avoiding Nuclear War

For the West a central objective is to achieve a stable security relationship with the Soviet Union. Our aspiration should be to continue to seek constructive forms of dialogue and cooperation with the USSR to reduce the risks of nuclear war, while preventing the Soviet Union from expanding its sphere of influence or engaging in military or political intimidation. More specifically, given the substantial Soviet military build-up, we must examine possible combinations of security and arms control decisions which can best maintain a military equilibrium within a continuing and fundamental rivalry between East and West.

Three major difficulties confront the trilateral world: hardware and balance sheet disequilibria between NATO and the Warsaw Pact, the danger of decoupling U.S. and European security, and disagreements within the West over the extension of NATO capabilities and alliance support to other parts of the globe where the Soviets threaten.

The current U.S.-Soviet military relationship can best be described as a strategically ambiguous equivalence, in which the United States leads the Soviets in warheads, is generally ahead in the precision of delivery systems, and quite probably also in operational reliability. The United States is also moving ahead in the new generation of cruise missiles, and will soon be ahead in terms of individually self-correcting ballistic missiles. By contrast, Soviet advantages lie with throw-weight, the number of missile launchers, and probably advantages in the relative survivability of its strategic forces, its population, and its political command.

These ambivalent dynamics have been matched by a more dangerous disequilibrium in relative defense expenditures. While the Soviets increased real defense spending by 3 to 4 per cent per year from the mid 1960s until the late 1970s, the U.S. sank $300 billion in 1982 dollars into Vietnam alone, and then actually decreased real spending from 1969 to 1977, when it again began to increase defense spending. Similarly, the Warsaw Pact military investment has exceeded that of NATO plus Japan since 1973, and is currently at least 15-20 percent larger.

Recent increases in U.S. defense expenditures have contributed to U.S.-EEC disagreements over the U.S. budget deficits as well as to equally divisive intra-U.S. squabbles over new missile systems such as the MX. Increasingly testy U.S. demands for greater financial participation in the common defense by the European NATO states have led to an extension until 1986 of the 5-year agreement on a 3 per cent per year real increase in defense expenditures undertaken in 1977, and a push for Japan to upgrade its defense capabilities before its public could comfortably accept it. Despite a second Five Year Plan to upgrade defense procurement from 1983 to 1987, Japan is still spending only 1 per cent of its GNP per annum on defense (1.5 per cent on the NATO definition). This fact is often linked by the U.S. public and on Capitol Hill with the $21 billion trade deficit with Japan, and it becomes yet another focus for resentment.

Regarding Western Europe, the problems have mushroomed. The second world war left the United States with global military responsibilities which its European allies had no capacity or desire to assume. But even within Europe there was a reluctance to increase defense expenditures, and a preference to make the risk of nuclear conflict so high to the Warsaw Pact that any conflict on German soil would carry unacceptable risks. European governments have not tried to persuade their populations that they really need a major conventional battle-fighting capability in order to change NATO's present strategy of early use of nuclear weapons through an affordable mix of conventional capability and a higher nuclear threshold. This would be more expensive but less of a nuclear risk. As a result they now face anti-nuclear protests on Pershing and cruise deployments, with an increasingly divided public opinion on the question of nuclear deterrence. However, the protesters as yet show little readiness to follow the logic of their position and support increased conventional forces spending.

Moreover, there is bound to be growing tension between the continuing need to enhance NATO's defense capabilities and the understandable German interest in furthering closer East-West German links. These tensions have until now proved manageable against a background of economic buoyancy and confidence in U.S. strategy and leadership. Deterioration of both economic buoyancy and strategic confidence is prompting widespread concern in Western Europe and stronger neutralist tendencies in West Germany itself, though the 1983 West German elections did decisively reject the neutralist option.

A further complication is the unpalatable fact that during the next decade it will be impossible to decouple U.S.-Soviet arms control efforts, which must continue, and the NATO-Warsaw Pact rivalry from some consideration of the French and British nuclear weapons in the East-West arms control talks. These weapons will soon involve hundreds of warheads. French forces alone by the 1990s will be capable of hitting several hundred major Soviet targets. It is difficult to imagine how U.S.-Soviet forces can be reciprocally scaled down without taking this new reality into account. Yet this could create serious problems within the alliance.

The division of Europe is resented by many West and East Europeans, with the German desire for closer national links serving as the major catalyst for change. How such change may occur will determine whether the relationship between the East and the West remains stable or becomes increasingly turbulent. It could also affect the cohesion of the Atlantic Alliance and thus the capacity of the trilateral countries to cooperate more effectively. At the same time, continued unrest in Poland, and an unsatisfactory economic and political situation, could spark upheavals which would obviously have unsettling consequences for East-West security.

Efforts by the trilateral countries to intensify their economic, scientific, and cultural ties with East Europe can contribute to gradually binding East and West Europe more closely, progressively undoing the division of Europe that has existed since 1945. Present tensions in East-West relations, notably between the United States and the Soviet Union, should not inhibit such efforts. Indeed over a longer period of time such efforts can also create the basis for a more wide-ranging pattern of economic relations with the Soviet Union itself while in the meantime contributing to the gradual undoing of the existing division of Europe. More specifically, in the case of Poland, selective lifting of some of the sanctions and limitations on contacts needs careful timing in order to sustain the basis for eventual internal liberalization.

The West will also need a proper mix of military strength and negotiating skill to deal with shifts in various regional balances and to counter Soviet forces and influence—not just in Europe, but also in the Persian Gulf, Pakistan, Afghanistan, the Far East and Africa. This means that the collective voice of Europe will have to be expressed on these matters, and Japan and Canada will certainly also wish to have their concerns fully reflected in any response by the United States which may affect their interests. While at this stage Japan is certainly not predisposed to join in a geopolitically wider alliance, nonetheless the historic import of the Williamsburg Declaration of 1983 was its acknowledgment of the interdependence of Japanese, European and North American security.

Regional Conflicts

Before the requisite unanimity of action can occur, trilateral consensus must be developed on the promotion and maintenance of regional security. It cannot be a unilateral U.S. decision.

A diversity of regional threats will confront humanity during the 1980s, often of a more dangerous kind than in the past. Regional conflicts over influence and territory will still occur, but they are likely to be complicated by sales of nuclear technology in conflict with non-proliferation objectives. Similarly, what were once indecisive conflicts of low priority to the West today increasingly draw the attention and support of major powers. Expended weapons are rapidly replaced by the major arms suppliers. Most of the West as well as the Soviets are to blame. The implications of that resupply are awesome: Third World purchases of arms from the industrialized world in 1980 were $44.2 billion, up $15 billion from 1979. The United States, France and the USSR were the three largest suppliers.

Nuclear proliferation, burgeoning arms sales, larger and better-equipped Third World armies and Soviet adventurism are by no means the only difficulties in terminating or containing regional conflicts in the next decade. Substantially different conceptions of security and legitimacy now exist in the world, which is composed of so many more nation-states. The problems for the international community of ensuring security for small states were illustrated by the coup in Grenada. In addition, frequently no common perception of a threat—or of its definition—exists within a given region and, more importantly, the criteria of threat tend to vary from one region to another.

Moreover, key regions such as Southern Africa, the Horn of Africa, and the Persian Gulf all face a broad spectrum of threats which require a highly differentiated set of responses. No clear theories for advance recognition, analysis and response to highly varied security threats have yet been developed and America's foreign policy has certainly not offered any practical evidence of one.

In the immediate future, major regional unrest is to be expected in the geopolitically sensitive regions of the Middle East, Central America and Eastern Europe. Each carries with it the possibility of heightened East-West tensions and even conflicts. While the shaping of a common trilateral approach on these regional issues may not prove possible, greater consultation and cooperation is clearly to be desired.

The Arab-Israeli conflict may be reaching the point of no return. If the annexation or colonization of the West Bank by Israel moves much further, Israel to survive will need to become a garrison state. The Arab world will be further radicalized and the Soviet Union will become more influential in the region.

Further progress on a resolution of the Arab-Israeli dispute linking Jordan with the West Bank along the lines outlined in President Reagan's speech of September 1, 1982 must be given a high priority, as must the stabilization of Lebanon. The multilateral peacekeeping effort in Beirut with French, U.S., Italian and British participation was a sign of a combined American and European willingness to shoulder some of the military and economic costs of security arrangements that would have to be contrived as part of a wider Israeli-Arab accommodation. Japan, with its dependence on Middle East oil, has a strong interest in a stable peace, and therefore should also be supportive of any such arrangements. By the same token, such involvement gives American allies the right to press the United States to use more firmly its political and economic leverage both on the Arab states and on Israel to make necessary concessions for peace. Whereas in the 1960s Europe and Japan were broadly content to see the United States try on its own to achieve a settlement of the Arab-Israeli dispute, that is no longer the case. The Middle East is thus one more troubled region which reveals the nature of trilateral interdependence.

Similarly, to the extent that the Central American issue threatens to involve the United States in a protracted conflict, with possibly very adverse consequences for U.S. relations with the southern hemisphere, its constructive resolution is very much in the interest of America's trilateral partners. An America beleaguered and bogged down in a crisis immediately south of its borders is likely to be an America less able to enhance trilateral cooperation and to promote trilateral security.

West Europe and Japan should give serious consideration to becoming associated—as Canada already is—with longer-term socio-economic development plans for the Central American and Caribbean regions. Such an engagement would be a natural extension of trilateral cooperation in Africa and Asia. It would build upon already existing Japanese aid packages to the Dominican Republic and Jamaica, as well as a long French, British, Spanish and Portuguese interest in the region. Moreover, such external assistance would mitigate the tendency in the United States to perceive the Central American problem purely as a Soviet-Cuban challenge and encourage the needed longer-range and more patient policy of both political and economic development.

Weakness in the Third World and the Institutional Challenge

The economic strains which many Third World governments are experiencing have already proved too great for many existing political structures to sustain. Some fear that we may be entering a period like the 1930s, when economic stress triggered 50 violent civil disturbances by 1933. The stability which the West has found in economic adversity is largely a product of a history of good times which provides hope for recovery, large governmental reserves which can be drawn upon to boost the economy, and a welfare state which protects individual citizens. Much of the late-developing Third World is bereft of all three of these critical protectors; faced with the anger of their disadvantaged populations, many governments may crack and break beneath the strain.

This weakness must be met by collective international action: through regional development organizations, governmental lending, Western investment, and private bank involvement. Latin America's successful Inter-American Development Bank and the Asian Development Bank provide important examples of regional programs which maintained project funding and continuity while weathering the recent recession. Likewise, worldwide organizations such as the IMF and the World Bank as well as the major bilateral donors will have to coordinate assistance to critical areas of special concern, such as Africa in general, food security, irrigation projects, deforestation, rural extension services, and alternative energy sources.

Africa's problems may be the world's worst. As early as 1981 the World Bank predicted that the net flow of outside aid into Africa would have to double by 1990 if average per capita incomes were to stop eroding and begin to increase again significantly. In addition, the United Nations Food and Agricultural Organization has warned that 22 of Africa's states "are facing catastrophic food shortages." Comparable in severity to the famine of 1973-74 which took hundreds of thousands of lives, the food shortages are much more widespread in that they now include Southern Africa as well, which has been suffering its worst drought in a century.

It is also worth recalling the world's vast disparity between the approximately $900 billion which is spent each year on arms, and the $30-40 billion invested in development aid. This imbalance, largely the consequence of the East-West rivalry, can contribute to massive social breakdowns in the Third World—from which both East and West will suffer. Some Third World states are themselves at fault—for they are becoming significant arms exporters themselves. Here the West may have some useful influence, since close ties link these regional powers with the West. Already, both Brazil and Israel sell more than $1 billion worth of arms each year, with Brazil disbursing to 16 countries and Israel to at least 18. South Korea, South Africa, Taiwan and Argentina are also major regional producers. The extraordinary increases in arms sales to Africa and Latin America in the past decade (Africa's expenditures alone jumped 13 times) reflect elite fears of internal insecurity more than external aggression. Yet the massive social programs which are needed to satisfy suffering populations are denuded by the Third

World's expenditures on arms, which have grown from $27 billion in 1970 to $117 billion in 1980.

Since it is unlikely that the Soviet bloc will measurably increase its developmental assistance, preferring military aid as it does, it becomes all the more incumbent upon the trilateral countries to increase their share. In this endeavor, the most likely constraint is the reluctance of trilateral electorates to fund development projects far from their shores, especially in states with regimes uncongenial to Western ideals of democracy and human rights.

CONCLUSION

Effecting any change in the international system—no matter how slight—will be exceedingly difficult. Short of a benevolent world dictatorship bent on reform, we must work within the bounds of an inefficient, adolescent international system, with all the pain, crisis, and irrationality which adolescence dictates. Since true consensus even within the two major power blocs occurs only on the most critical of issues, and then often on nothing but the identification of a problem, our necessary point of departure must be to place greater emphasis on improving the performance of existing international machinery. We should not be blind to the substantial promise inherent in bringing the functioning of existing institutions up to their true potential, though we also recognize the need for some additional forms of enhanced trilateral cooperation.

We must also come to terms with the implications of a simple reality. For the trilateral countries to be able to cope with the problems discussed and to pursue effectively their goals for the decade, two fundamental preconditions must be satisfied:
- a wider economic recovery must be sustained
- a strategic and conventional military balance with Soviet bloc forces must be maintained.

Each of these two broad preconditions will require major effort and sacrifice. To maintain an adequate military balance, given the momentum of the Soviet effort, the NATO countries will have to fulfill their earlier commitment to increase defense spending by a significant amount each year, and Japan should associate itself with this undertaking even if it decides to make its contribution through development aid rather than military expenditure.

There is simply no escape from this painful fact. Sacrifice and self-denial will be needed. It will require dedicated and courageous political leadership.

V. Tasks and Trade-Offs: The Trilateral Response

If the problems discussed earlier in this report are to be effectively tackled, the trilateral countries must adopt a specific, action-oriented agenda, and start to take urgent steps to put it into effect. The obvious forum for agreement on such an agenda is the series of annual economic summits to be held over the next few years. No single summit meeting will be able to solve all these problems: each summit will need to monitor developments and decide on fresh action in the light of experience. Moreover, the summit discussions will need to be extended beyond the economic matters with which they have hitherto been mainly concerned to encompass other issues relating to the effective working of democracy, political stability and military security discussed in this report. We believe that the concept of a comprehensive, rather than simply an economic summit should be adopted and a decision taken to call them henceforth Strategic or Policy Summits.

Crucial to our perception of a satisfactory political agenda for our countries over the next decade is the notion of trade-offs. Many of the steps that need to be taken will involve hard political choices and will be unpopular with some sections of our domestic electorates. If governments are to take such steps, they must have the assurance not only that other governments are taking necessary, if unpopular, action as well, but also that the costs to their own people of the action they themselves are taking are likely to be out-weighed by the benefits that accrue to them from the actions of others. There must, in short, be a system of trade-offs, in which each government agrees to take action it might prefer to avoid, in return for the advantages which the actions taken by other governments will bring to it. Such a system would make every country better off than if each government abstained from taking unpopular decisions.

The best model for such a set of trade-offs is probably the summit held in Bonn in 1978. On that occasion all the participants agreed to take various actions which, left to themselves, they might have shirked, in order to promote the common good. The United States agreed to adopt various anti-inflationary measures and to raise its domestic oil prices to world market levels by the end of 1980. This crucial decision was politically possible only in the context of the summit agreement. Germany promised action to raise GNP by one per cent. Japan undertook to expand domestic demand so as to increase the growth of total output by 1.5 per cent, and temporarily to avoid any increase in the volume of its exports. France agreed to increase its budget deficit by 0.5 per cent of GNP; Canada and Italy undertook to increase their growth rates; and Britain pointed out that it had very recently applied a fiscal stimulus of over one per cent of GNP. It is worth remembering that at the same time a collective NATO decision to increase defense spending by three per cent in real terms each year had been agreed.

It became fashionable a few years later to decry the effects of the decisions taken at the Bonn summit; expressions of regret came in particularly from Germany and Japan. In our view this reaction is largely misconceived. It is true that at the time of the summit the expansionary forces already at work in the world economy may have been underestimated, and that, with hindsight, it might have been appropriate to apply a slightly more modest stimulus. But the inflationary and balance of payments problems experienced by Germany and Japan in 1979 and 1980 were much less the result of the measures they had agreed to at Bonn than of the more than doubling of oil prices in 1979-80 triggered by the Iranian civil war—a series of developments that could hardly have been foreseen in mid-1978. It is not surprising that more recently there has been a shift of opinion back in favor of the kind of approach adopted at Bonn, or that some of the leading participants themselves—some of whom at one time openly regretted the measures they had agreed to take—should by the spring of 1983 be vigorously—though unsuccessfully—advocating that a similar approach be adopted at the May 1983 summit at Williamsburg.

At the present time it seems to us that there are six tasks that need to be undertaken by the trilateral countries as a matter of urgency and which should be the concern of forthcoming summits. Some call for action by particular trilateral countries or regions; others require action by all. But they should be regarded as a single package, and undertaken simultaneously, not only to maximize their economic effects, but because it is politically realistic to expect individual governments to tackle some of these problems with the necessary vigor only if the other problems are being tackled as well, so that they have an assurance that the costs of their own actions are likely to be more than compensated by the benefits they receive from the actions of others. We have no illusions that this process will be easy, or that the bargains will be automatic and evenly balanced. We also recognize that the trade-offs will need to be carefully monitored by subsequent summits, and may need adjustment in the light of experience.

We list and briefly discuss each of these six tasks below, focusing first on the main problem which needs to be tackled in each trilateral region, and then on three issues which must engage the attention of all trilateral countries equally.

ACTION BY INDIVIDUAL TRILATERAL PARTNERS

1. The United States must take urgent action to reduce its budget deficit. This is now running at an annual rate of about $200 billion, or 5.5 per cent of GNP, compared with an average of 1.5 per cent of GNP over the period 1965-80. On present policies, the deficit seems unlikely to fall below five per cent of GNP over the next few years.

The combination of these large fiscal deficits and the relatively restrictive monetary policy pursued by the Federal Reserve has resulted—in a country in which the personal savings ratio is low—in real interest rates which are, by historical standards, still very high, though nominal rates have dropped. So far, the damage done by these high interest rates in the United States itself appears to be limited, partly because individual, as well as business, borrowers still obtain relatively large tax reliefs on interest payments, and partly because the recent sharp recovery of the economy has led to a surge in company profits and cash flow. But it seems highly likely that the financing of a continuing budget deficit of five per cent or more of the GNP will before long start to crowd out private investment on an increasing scale. In the medium term this will have adverse effects on the growth of productivity in the American economy; in the short term it could bring the recovery to a halt, and subsequently could plunge the economy back into recession.

Abroad the effects of the U.S. budget deficit have already been severe. Other developed countries have been forced to maintain high interest rates in order to limit the depreciation of their currencies against the dollar, and this has held back the recovery of their own economies. Developing countries with a large burden of external debt have been doubly hit: their debt is having to be serviced at high rates of interest and—being mainly denominated in dollars—at unfavorable exchange rates.

A further adverse consequence of the U.S. deficit and the high interest rates to which it has led stems from the large appreciation of the dollar which has taken place over the last three years, and which has left the dollar seriously overvalued. One effect of the attendant decline in U.S. competitiveness both at home and abroad has been the emergence of a balance of payments deficit on current account which in

1984 may represent as much as two per cent of GNP—in itself a serious problem. But the other effect is even more worrying: the impetus given to protectionist forces within the United States by the increasing difficulty American manufactures are experiencing in competing with imports. If America were really to revert to protectionism, the outlook for the world economy would be grim indeed.

We do not presume to prescribe in any detail the combination of expenditure cuts and tax increases that the United States should adopt: that is for Americans to decide. But it does seem to us that one element in a desirable package would be some reduction in the growth rate of defense expenditure—an adjustment that might be both politically and militarily more acceptable if some of our other related security recommendations regarding Western Europe and Japan are adopted. Another might be some reduction in the real value of the federal entitlements where they go to people who are far from being the neediest members of the population. As far as taxation is concerned, one possibility would be to suspend the indexation of tax thresholds; another would be to introduce a comprehensive energy tax. The precise combination of measures adopted is not important; what is important is that something be done, and done soon. We recognize the difficulties that any Administration must have in taking unpopular decisions to raise taxes or cut expenditures in an election year. But an expressed readiness to collectively undertake a series of measures will be a precondition for the development of a coordinated summit package. Canada, like the United States, is running a large structural budget deficit, but its reduction would be of no great international significance. It may be more important for Canada to increase either its defense expenditure, which is relatively low, or its aid expenditure, which is relatively high, but still below the O.7 per cent United Nations target.

2. Europe must take radical action to adapt faster to a rapidly changing environment. In two particular respects, the outlook for Europe is threatening. In some important fields—though not in all—it is technologically backward compared with the United States and Japan, and in some cases this backwardness shows signs of becoming more pronounced. And it is suffering from unemployment on a more extensive and persistent scale than either of its trilateral partners. These two problems, left unsolved, could before long challenge the postwar stability of Europe and the strategic and international consensus that has developed within the framework of NATO and the European Community.

The problem of technological backwardness must be tackled on a number of fronts. The forces of competition within Europe itself must be strengthened: the still-existing artificial barriers to genuine free trade, and to public procurement in the cheapest European market, must be swept aside. Subsidies to older industries which have lost their comparative advantage to their expanding counterparts in the newly industrializing countries must be phased out more swiftly and more decisively. These are decisions which should be taken on their merits by the European Community. The Common Agricultural Policy is the cement of the European Economic Community and must be made to operate more efficiently. The first priority is to reduce surplus production. Subsidies to exports of European farm produce to other countries are a source of friction with the United States and Canada and eventually must be eliminated; but it is unrealistic to demand that this be done immediately, particularly in view of of the strains that the admission of Spain and Portugal will put on the Common Agricultural Policy. The immediate action for the Community, which is tolerable, is to halt all steel and other industrial subsidies.

Above all, Europe must get back into the vanguard of technological advance on a wider front: it must seize on the opportunities offered by the microelectronic revolution. One priority here is greater collaboration with the Japanese or North American firms which are at the frontier of the high-tech developments of the late 1980s and 1990s: in particular, joint ventures in which Japanese capital and technology are combined with European skills to produce the goods and services of the future could be of benefit to both regions. Another way forward—not inconsistent with the first—would involve much greater rationalization of industry on a Europe-wide scale, so that a plethora of national firms would give way to a smaller number of large European firms, with unrestricted access to the markets of all Western European countries, and able to compete on equal terms with leading North American and Japanese companies.

The second European problem—persistent high unemployment, particularly among the young—will be easier to cope with, after a transitional period, if Europe vigorously pursues the sort of measures discussed above: failure to adapt to the new technologies will destroy far more jobs in the longer run than adapting to them will. Even so, the record suggests that it may be optimistic to suppose that faster growth or a greater spirit of dynamism in Western Europe will of themselves solve the unemployment problem; over the last 20 years the EEC has created very little increase in the number of people employed, whereas in North America over the same period employment rose by around 35 million, or nearly 50 per cent. Unemployment in Europe may only be brought down to acceptable levels if the next few years also witness the beginning of a systematic move towards a shorter working life for those in employment, whether through longer periods of education and training, a shorter working week, longer annual holidays, earlier retirement, or some combination of these. In the age of the computer and the robot, existing patterns of paid employment will change, and a start should be made—in North America and Japan, as well as in Europe—on adapting the length and structure of working life to the characteristics of the post-industrial era.

3. Japan must increasingly come to play a bigger role in the world which is commensurate with its economic power and its performance at the frontiers of technological advance. We envisage four particular ways in which it might do this.

First, it must take measures to expand its economy at a faster rate, thus helping to stimulate world economic growth. Secondly, as a country with a high personal savings ratio and a tendency to run sizeable balance of payments surpluses on current account, it is appropriate that Japan should assume a role as a steady and significant exporter of capital. It would be particularly valuable for the health of the trilateral community as a whole if a good deal of the overseas investment financed by this outflow of capital were to be located in Western Europe in the form of projects—undertaken in some cases in cooperation with European companies—which employed the latest Japanese technology. This would help Europe to narrow the technological gap which has opened up between it and its trilateral partners, and at the same time assist with the creation of new European jobs. Japan would benefit by maintaining access to markets that might otherwise become increasingly closed to it by the protectionist measures that could well be forced on European governments by an ever-rising tide of goods imported from Japan.

Thirdly, Japan should take positive steps towards the internationalization of the yen, and the liberalization of its financial and capital markets.

Finally, it is highly desirable that Japan should make a greater contribution to the kind of expenditures designed to promote a more peaceful and prosperous world. It could, for example, assume a significantly greater share of the burden of defending our common interests against external aggression: at present it spends one per cent of its GNP on defense—or 1.5 per cent on the NATO definition—compared with seven per cent for the United States, around four per cent for the major

Western European countries, and two per cent for Canada. If, however, political considerations and the susceptibilities of its neighbors make it injudicious for Japan to engage in a big defense build-up, it must instead increase the assistance it provides to needy Third World countries. It should concentrate on those Third World countries whose stability is of special strategic importance to the defense interests of the trilateral democracies. At present, Japanese official development assistance to developing countries represents only about 0.3 per cent of GNP—a slightly higher figure than for the United States but significantly lower than for most Western European countries and Canada. But any increase in ODA must not simply lead to an expansion of Japanese exports through tied aid, or even some day by arms sales.

There are a number of ways of avoiding these consequences. Japan could provide extra funding for the IMF in the way that Saudi Arabia, for example, has done. It should increase its bilateral aid to developing countries or increase the resources it makes available to the World Bank and to the International Development Association (IDA)—an institution whose prospective shortage of funds threatens horrendous consequences in several of the poorest parts of the world. A significant contribution would be three billion dollars over three years, making up the shortfall in the seventh IDA replenishment.

There is no shortage of ways in which Japan could help Third World countries if it were willing to make more resources available. Given the size and rate of growth of the Japanese economy, and the relatively limited contribution it makes to both defense and aid programs at the moment, it is important that Japan makes an early commitment to the provision of substantially increased resources for these purposes in a manner that would be seen as taking over a part of the existing U.S. and to a lesser extent Western Europe's global expenditure commitments.

JOINT ACTION BY THE TRILATERAL PARTNERS

1. Sustained non-inflationary economic growth is needed if the problem of unemployment is to be brought under control, and if the international debt problem is to be contained and eventually resolved. Economic growth in the OECD countries as a whole for the rest of the decade of anything under three per cent is unlikely, as judged by a number of international studies, to meet these requirements; something closer to four per cent ought to be aimed at.

Coordination of economic policies is needed because the world has become so interdependent that economic policies which are formulated without regard to their effects on other countries are likely to have undesirable consequences. We have already pointed to the adverse effects on other countries of the large U.S. budget deficit. Similarly, the restrictive fiscal and monetary policies pursued by such countries as Britain and West Germany in recent years have had deflationary effects on other countries, which have in turn reacted in ways that have further slowed down the growth of international trade and world output. An example of a different kind is France, which in 1981 was virtually alone in adopting expansionary policies, but stagnation elsewhere meant that its rising imports were not offset by rising exports. Only if the main trilateral countries discuss their proposed economic policies with each other, and are prepared to modify them to some extent in order to promote the common good, is it likely, in our judgment, that sustained economic expansion will be achieved.

A particular area where policy coordination is essential is in the field of exchange rates. At the present time exchange rates are clearly in a state of fundamental disequilibrium, with the dollar very significantly overvalued and other currencies, particularly the Deutschmark and the yen, undervalued. Only appropriate domestic economic policies—including a reduction in the U.S. budget deficit—are likely to bring exchange rates back into reasonable alignment. But once such alignment is achieved, we favor regular monitoring of exchange rate developments by the main trilateral countries, and policy action—including coordinated intervention in the foreign exchange markets by the authorities if necessary—in order to ensure that the main currencies are kept in a reasonable relationship to each other. A system of flexible "target zones" and a specific mechanism for triggering consultation between the five governments in the Versailles group, the U.S., France, Germany, Britain, and Japan, designed to prevent individual currencies from moving outside these zones, seem to us important ingredients in avoiding the costs of both the volatility and the misalignment of currencies that have been witnessed since generalized floating began in 1973.

2. The cost of defense must be more equally shared among the trilateral countries. That the United States spends a significantly larger portion of its GNP on defense than any other trilateral country has two particular disadvantages. One is that heavy American defense expenditures are a significant factor in its large budget deficit. Since President Reagan took office, defense expenditure has been rising rapidly. It was originally projected to rise from 5.3 per cent of GNP in 1981 to 5.7 per cent in 1982 and to 7.9 per cent in 1985. However, the $306 billion fiscal 1985 budget request unveiled in January 1984 is up 13 per cent from fiscal 1984. That 13 per cent increase for fiscal 1985 is on top of a 12

per cent increase in fiscal year 1982, an eight per cent increase in fiscal 1983, and a four per cent increase in 1984. Military spending in 1985 will amount to 6.8 per cent of GNP. Clearly, anything which persuades the United States Administration to slow down the growth of its defense expenditure will be a helpful element in the crucial task of reducing the budget deficit. And if America's allies, including Canada, do more, America can afford to do less. The desirability of Japan increasing its strategic spending has already been mentioned. But whatever happens, an extra defense burden must be borne by Western Europe. Europe must in return be able to produce more defense equipment to ensure not just more jobs, but also to boost technological development. It is unrealistic to expect European politicians to convince their electorates of the need to commit more resources to conventional defense if a 10:1 procurement imbalance continues between the United States and Europe.

There is a second argument for transferring some part of the existing defense burden from the United States to Europe. There is growing unease in Western Europe about the nuclear arms race, and in particular about nuclear weapons strategy in Europe, and the prospect that NATO might feel it had no alternative, in the event of a conventional invasion from the East, to the early use of these nuclear weapons. If a greater European defense commitment were to take the form of a strengthening of its conventional forces, the prospects of ever having to use nuclear weapons would be reduced, and some of the main sources of tension between the United States and its European allies removed. In 1986, NATO's commitment to three per cent annual increases in defense spending in real terms ends, and it is vital that well before this Western Europe agrees to a long-term commitment to increase its conventional defense effort.

3. A method must be devised of coping with the international debt problem. So far, this has been dealt with by a series of ad hoc reschedulings. It is possible that this approach will continue to be successful in the future, particularly if interest rates come down, if there is a fall in the value of the dollar and if the world economy achieves reasonably rapid and sustained economic growth. In these favorable circumstances, debtor countries should by and large be able to service their external debt without imposing undue hardships on their own people. But it would be unwise to assume that things will go this well. The possibility of moratoria or defaults by one or two major countries, which might then be copied by many others, cannot be ruled out.

The responsibility for the precarious structure of international debt which has been built up over the past decade rests partly with the developing countries which borrowed too much, partly with the international private banks which lent too much, and partly with the governments of the trilateral countries which gave too much encouragement to this excessive process of borrowing and lending. Correspondingly, each group must expect to bear some of the costs of resolving the problem in a controlled and systematic way. The debtor countries must expect to suffer some hardship as the debt is serviced. The banks must expect to have to use some of their profits to strengthen their capital base, and to reconcile themselves to many delays in repayment, and perhaps some defaults. And the taxpayers of the developed countries must expect to pick up some of the bill in the form of increased resources made available to the international financial institutions such as the IMF, the World Bank, and the Regional Development Banks.

It is this last obligation that the trilateral countries must agree to undertake. The IMF, in particular, must be provided with the necessary resources to enable it to support debtor countries which need time to service their debts and cannot rely on the private banking system alone for an adequate response to their difficulties. At the same time the IMF itself will need to interpret its terms of reference more flexibly than at present to deal with cases in which the conventional criteria would deny adequate assistance to key countries whose political or strategic importance to the West means that they cannot be allowed to go into default on their debt or to slide into internal anarchy and chaos.

A PACKAGE DEAL

These six tasks need to be tackled simultaneously. Success in undertaking each task will make it easier to achieve success in undertaking the others. The process will be mutually supportive: the whole will be greater than the sum of the parts. Success in reducing the budget deficit in the United States, for example, by leading to lower interest rates and a fall in the value of the dollar, will give a fillip to other industrial countries: lower import prices in terms of domestic currency will help to contain inflation, while lower interest rates will help to boost investment.

Lower interest rates and a lower dollar will also ease the burden of debt servicing for developing countries and enable them to pursue more expansionary policies than would otherwise be possible. The United States will find it easier to reduce its budget deficit—by cutting back the growth of defense expenditure—if Europe undertakes to increase its conventional military expenditures so as to shoulder a greater proportion of the burden of defending the West against external aggression. Although Japan may feel unable to increase its defense expenditure significantly, a substantial increase in its grants and loans to the Third World would help everybody by increasing the stability and prosperity of key parts of the globe. Correspondingly, an increased flow of Japanese capital and technology to Europe would help Europe to adapt to new technological developments, and to cope with its severe unemployment problem. Faster growth and higher employment in Europe would, in turn, reduce the dangers of protectionist measures to keep out Japanese imports, just as a reduction in agricultural and industrial subsidies in Europe would lessen the likelihood of protectionist sentiment gaining ground in the United States.

In short, the kind of package of trade-offs we advocate above is one from which everyone would benefit. Accordingly, we strongly urge that forthcoming summits take as their objective the detailed development of such a package. In particular we recommend that a NATO meeting at Heads of Government level be scheduled for early 1985, to affirm new forward defense expenditure commitments; and we recommend that an early special meeting of the IDA be convened at Finance Minister level. The successful achievement of the tasks contained in our initial summit package should be the main concern of subsequent summits.

There is much concern within the industrialized democracies about the disjunction in policy-making that has taken place when democratic elections lead to changes of government. This is of particular concern in relation to the United States, whose international weight makes policy changes particularly disruptive. This effect is to some extent the inevitable and broadly beneficial consequence of democracy, but the summit process does have the potential to moderate the wider swings of policy through the maintenance of an international consensus, and by persuading governments to fulfill commitments entered into as a result of a trade-off process engaged in by their predecessors.

OUR WIDER AGENDA

The historical significance of our trilateral relationship is that our countries are genuine pioneers in forging socially just democracies and in shaping a wider and more equitable system of international cooperation. To play this role effectively we must be guided by an enlightened vision of the future, by a sense of shared purpose beyond today's crises. Our report, therefore, outlines also an action agenda for the rest of the decade—an agenda designed to give substance to our shared values. It is our view—as developed in the substantive chapters—that our trilateral countries should seek to formulate common and more detailed programs:

- to achieve, on a sustainable basis, faster rates of economic growth and productivity increase than have been achieved over the past five years;
- to reduce structural unemployment and to increase skill training;
- to facilitate increased leisure and work-sharing as one method of minimizing the worst aspects of unemployment;
- to encourage joint investment in technologically advanced industries so as to minimize current imbalances in trilateral development;
- to concentrate social provision on those most in need, taking into account the aging of our populations;
- to strengthen the international institutions crucial to continued world growth and development, such as the IMF, the World Bank group, and GATT;
- to develop a wider approach to East-West arms control negotiations, including the French and British strategic forces, and eventually also the Chinese;
- to engage in more systematic and binding trilateral consultations on a common approach to the important regional problems of the Middle East, Latin America, and Eastern Europe;
- to enlarge the scope and machinery for Atlantic-Pacific consultations by gradually drawing into these consultations other Asian nations, including China;
- to examine the possibility of special economic inducements to Third World countries so that they refrain from policies that produce nuclear proliferation or cause ecological devastation.

Some of these are matters best dealt with by governments. Some could well be subjects for more systematic study by organizations such as the Trilateral Commission. All of them should be guided by one shared principle: that democracy can and must work.

The Authors

DAVID OWEN is a Member of the British Parliament and leader of the Social Democratic Party. He is a former Labour Foreign Secretary.

Educated as a physician, Dr. Owen was first elected to Parliament (Labour) in 1966. He was Under Secretary of State for the Royal Navy from 1968 to 1970, before becoming Minister of State in the Department of Health and Social Security in 1974, a post which he retained until 1976, when he became Minister of State at the Foreign and Commonwealth Office, responsible for European Community affairs. He was appointed Secretary of State for Foreign and Commonwealth Affairs in February 1977 and retained the post until the General Election in May 1979.

Dr. Owen was one of the four founder members of the Council for Social Democracy which was set up in January 1981 and developed into the new Social Democratic Party, launched in March 1981. He became leader of the Party in June 1983.

Dr. Owen was a member of the Independent Commission on Disarmament and Security Issues, under the chairmanship of Mr. Olof Palme. He is the author of *The Politics of Defense* (1972); *In Sickness and In Health—The Politics of Medicine* (1976); *Human Rights* (1978) and *Face the Future* (1981).

SABURO OKITA, former Japanese Foreign Minister and Government Representative for External Economic Relations, is now Chairman of the Institute for Domestic and International Policy Studies, which he founded in March 1981. He is also advisor to the Ministry of Foreign Affairs, the Economic Planning Agency, and several other government agencies and research centers. He has been President of the International University of Japan since 1982.

Born in Manchuria, Dr. Okita graduated from Tokyo University in 1937 as an electrical engineer and entered government service. In 1956, he was appointed Director-General of the Planning Bureau of the Economic Planning Agency and participated inthe preparation of the famous "Doubling of National Income Plan" in 1960. He left the EPA in 1963 to become President and then Chairman of the Japan Economic Research Center. He was President of the Overseas Economic Cooperation Fund from 1973 to 1977.

Dr. Okita has been involved in a multitude of international activities, including member of the U.N. Committee for Development Planning (1965-1980) and member of the World Bank's Commission on International Development (Pearson Commission, 1968-69).

Dr. Okita is the author of many articles in English and of a dozen books in Japanese on Japan's economy, Asian economic development, international relations, etc. His latest books in English are *Developing Economies and Japan—Lessons in Growth* (1980) and *Japan's Challenging Years—Reflections on My Lifetime* (1983).

ZBIGNIEW BRZEZINSKI is Herbert Lehman Professor of Government at Columbia University and Senior Advisor at the Georgetown University Center for Strategic and International Studies.

Dr. Brzezinski was born in Poland and moved to North America before the Second World War. He was educated at McGill University and Harvard University (Ph.D., 1953). He taught at Harvard from 1953 until 1960, when he moved to Columbia University. In 1966-68 he served as a member of the Policy Planning Council of the U.S. State Department, and in 1968 he directed the Foreign Policy Task Forces for Vice President Humphrey's Presidential campaign. He was a founder of the Trilateral Commission and its first Director from 1973 to 1976.

In 1977, he joined the Administration of President Jimmy Carter, as Assistant to the President for National Security Affairs, a post he held throughout the Administration. In 1981, Dr. Brzezinski assumed his current teaching and research posts at Georgetown and Columbia.

Among his numerous publications are *Alternative to Partition: For a Broader Conception of America's Role in Europe* (1965), *Between Two Ages: America's Role in the Technetronic Era* (1970), *The Fragile Blossom: Crisis and Change in Japan* (1972), and *Power and Principle* (1983).

The Trilateral Process

The report which follows is the joint responsibility of the three authors, with David Owen serving as principal author. Although only the authors are responsible for the analysis and conclusions, they have been aided in their work by many others.

The authors are particularly indebted to their associates for this project. On the European side, Michael Stewart was David Owen's associate. Mr. Stewart spent a number of years as an economist in Whitehall, in particular with the Treasury, Cabinet Office, Foreign Office, and 10 Downing Street. Educated at Magdalen College, Oxford (first-class degree in Philosophy, Politics, and Economics), he is now Reader in Political Economy at University College, London. His most recent book is *Controlling the Economic Future: Policy Dilemmas in a Shrinking World* (1983).

On the North American side, Carol Rae Hansen was Zbigniew Brzezinski's associate. Ms. Hansen, a Ph.D. candidate in political science at Harvard University, joined Dr. Brzezinski's staff in 1982. In the previous five years, she had a range of assignments with the U.S. government—with the National Security Council staff, the C.I.A., the State Department, and the Department of Agriculture. Her previous higher education was at Augustana College and the Johns Hopkins School of Advanced International Studies.

On the Japanese side, Saburo Okita was particularly assisted by Charles Morrison and Masahiro Sakamoto. Dr. Morrison is concurrently Research Fellow at the Japan Center for International Exchange and at the East-West Center in Honolulu. Mr. Sakamoto, formerly with the Economic Planning Agency (EPA), is now Chief Economist for the Japan International Trade Institute. He was seconded from EPA to the OECD in Paris in the late 1970s for work in the Interfutures Project.

In addition to these individuals, the authors consulted a wide range of other persons—in and out of government—in the course of their work. The first full authors' meeting was in London in July 1983. In October, David Owen discussed the project at the European regional meeting in Lisbon. The second authors' meeting was in Washington on December 1-2, where discussion centered on first drafts of Chapters II,

III, and IV, and the shape of Chapter V. A full draft was discussed at the third authors' meeting in Tokyo on January 30-31, which led to a revised draft a few weeks later. This revised draft was distributed in March to members of the Trilateral Commission and was discussed at the Commission's annual plenary in Washington on April 2, 1984. A final draft was produced shortly thereafter.